**PROTOCOLS FOR
POSTCAPITALIST EXPRESSION**

AGENCY, FINANCE AND SOCIALITY IN THE NEW ECONOMIC SPACE

Dick Bryan, Jorge López & Akseli Virtanen

ECONOMIC SPACE AGENCY

<.:.Min0r.:.>
.c0mp0siti0ns.

Protocols for Postcapitalist Expression. Agency, Finance and Sociality in the New Economic Space
Dick Bryan, Jorge López & Akseli Virtanen

ISBN 978-1-57027-414-5

Cover design by Pablo Somonte Ruano
Interior design by Casandra Johns (www.houseofhands.net)

Released by Minor Compositions 2023
Colchester / New York / Port Watson

Minor Compositions is a series of interventions & provocations drawing from autonomous politics, avant-garde aesthetics, and the revolutions of everyday life.

Minor Compositions is an imprint of Autonomedia
www.minorcompositions.info | minorcompositions@gmail.com

Distributed by Autonomedia
PO Box 568 Williamsburgh Station
Brooklyn, NY 11211

www.autonomedia.org
info@autonomedia.org

TABLE OF CONTENTS

LIST OF FIGURES 7
ACKNOWLEDGMENT 8
FOREWORD 9
    ON ECONOMIC INTELLIGENCE 9
    POSTCAPITALIST FUTURES 10
    THE REVALUATION OF VALUE 20
CHAPTER 1: INTRODUCTION 24
    1.1 CONTESTING THE CURRENT ORDER 24
    1.2 WHAT DOES THE FUTURE HOLD? 29
    1.3 A NEW ECONOMIC SPACE; NEW ECONOMIC PERFORMANCES 33
    1.4 A NOTE ON TERMINOLOGY 36
    1.5 CAPITALIST AND POSTCAPITALIST FINANCE 38
    1.6 THE IMMEDIATE PROPOSAL: LIVING IN THE SPREAD 42
APPENDIX 1.1: DESIGN PRINCIPLES OF THE NEW ECONOMIC SPACE 44
APPENDIX 1.2: SOME KEY DISTINCTIONS BETWEEN THE ECONOMIC SPACE PROTOCOL AND OTHER PARADIGMATIC BLOCKCHAIN ARCHITECTURES ... 46
    SECRECY VERSUS PRIVACY 46
CHAPTER 2: FROM CAPITALIST TO POSTCAPITALIST ECONOMY 48
    2.1 DESIGNING AN ECONOMY 48
    2.2 AN ECONOMICS PRIMER 49
    2.3 THE HAYEKIAN TURN: KNOWLEDGE, PRICE AND SPONTANEOUS ORDER 51
    2.4 HAYEK'S DEAD END 54
    2.5 PRICES FREED FROM PROFIT 58
    2.6 TURNING HAYEK ON HIS HEAD 60
    2.7 IMPLICATIONS 64
APPENDIX 2.1: DO 'BIG DATA' CHANGE THE STORY? 65
CHAPTER 3: MARKETS AS COMMUNICATION NETWORKS 68
    3.1 INTRODUCTION 68
    3.2 AGENTS AND MARKETS 70
    3.3 ECONOMIC SPACE 72
    3.4 TOKENS AND DISTRIBUTED LEDGERS 72
    3.5 WAYS OF 'PRICING' 74

3.6 PEER-TO-PEER; DECENTRALIZED TO DISTRIBUTED 75
3.7 SOCIAL OBJECTIVES. 76
3.8 GOVERNANCE 78
3.9 THE TOOLS TO REFRAME 79
CHAPTER 4: PRODUCTION AS PERFORMANCE. 81
4.1 BACKGROUND 81
4.2 PERFORMING RELATIONS. 82
4.3 PROTOCOLS OF PERFORMANCES 83
4.4 PERFORMANCE INDICES AND VALUE MEASURES 86
4.5 A 'VALUE THEORY OF PERFORMANCE' 88
APPENDIX 4.1: A PERFORMANCE EVALUATION FRAMEWORK 91
SOCIAL IMPACT BONDS 91
POLICY EVALUATION FRAMEWORK. 93
APPENDIX 4.2 95
PERFORMANCES (P) AND THEIR OUTPUTS (C) 95
SIMPLE COMMODITY PRODUCTION 95
CUMULATIVE COMMODITY PRODUCTION. 95
CHAPTER 5: STAKE: THE KEY TO VALUE 99
5.1 INTRODUCTION 99
5.2 THE CIRCULAR LOGIC OF RECIPROCAL STAKING 101
5.3 RETURNS TO STAKEHOLDING 105
5.4 STAKING AND THE NETWORK: A SUMMARY AND A PROJECTION. . . . 106
**APPENDIX 5.1: FUNDAMENTAL VALUE AND SPECULATION:
KEYNES' BEAUTY CONTEST 108**
APPENDIX 5.2: DIVIDENDS AND THE SURPLUS. 112
CHAPTER 6: THE COMMONS 116
6.1 FINDING THE COMMONS 116
6.2 RECIPROCAL STAKING FORMS THE 'SYNTHETIC COMMONS' 117
6.3 DIVIDENDS AS THE COMMON PURPOSE 117
6.4 THE COMMONS AS A PROCESS OF REDISTRIBUTION. 119
CHAPTER 7: POSTCAPITALIST UNITS OF MEASUREMENT. 121
7.1 INTRODUCTION 121
7.2 MEASUREMENT CATEGORIES FOR THE ECONOMIC
    SPACE PROTOCOL 122

7.3 POSTCAPITALIST UNITS OF VALUE................................125
7.4 CONCLUSION: BASIC CATEGORIES 129
CHAPTER 8: LIQUIDITY AND CREDIT..................................130
   8.1 INTRODUCTION...130
   8.2 THE GENERAL CONDITIONS OF DISTRIBUTED CREDIT ISSUANCE....131
   8.3 STAKE AS COLLATERAL: THE FOUNDATION OF CREDIT...........133
   8.4 NETWORK RECOGNITION OF CREDIT AND CREDIT SETTLEMENT....134
   8.5 IMPLICATIONS..136
APPENDIX 8.1: KEYNES ON MONEY AND CREDIT 138
CHAPTER 9: EXCHANGE RELATIONS EXPRESSED THROUGH TOKENS.....141
   9.1 CONTEXT 141
   9.2 RECIPROCAL ISSUANCE: OFFERS AND MATCHING................142
   9.3 NETTING AND CLEARING..144
   9.4 ECONOMIES ENABLED BY PROTOCOLS 146
APPENDIX 9.1: TOKENS AND NETWORK DERIVATIVES 147
CHAPTER 10: TOKENS AND LEDGERS 149
   10.1 INTRODUCTION 149
   10.2 STAKE TOKENS 150
   10.3 LIQUIDITY TOKENS 152
   10.4 COMMODITY TOKENS 155
   10.5 EXCHANGES BETWEEN TOKENS............................157
   10.6 THREE TOKEN CATEGORIES TO SERVE THREE
       ECONOMIC FUNCTIONS 159
CHAPTER 11: DYNAMICS OF A TOKENIZED NETWORK..................161
   11.1 THREE CIRCUITS OF VALUE 161
   11.2 THE PERFORMANCE CIRCUIT: THE CIRCUIT OF
       VALUE CREATION...163
   11.3 THE COLLATERAL CIRCUIT: THE CIRCUIT OF GROWTH..........165
   11.4 THE CREDIT CIRCUIT: THE CIRCUIT OF STABILITY 166
   11.5 SIGNIFICANCE..167
CHAPTER 12: STABILITY, VOLATILITY AND VALUE 168
   12.1 STABILITY 168
   12.2 OUTSIDE CURRENCY WITHIN THE NETWORK..................169
   12.3 VOLATILITY 170

APPENDIX 12.1: TOKENIZED VALUE: SIMPLE AND EXPANDED **173**
**APPENDIX 12.2: MV=PQ: AN APPLICATION TO THE
ECONOMIC SPACE PROTOCOL TOKEN LOGIC** **175**
**CHAPTER 13: THE CONDITIONS OF A DIGITAL
POSTCAPITALIST ECONOMY** **178**
    13.1 INTRODUCTION 178
    13.2 NETWORK VALUE 179
    13.3 WHERE TO FROM HERE? 181
BIBLIOGRAPHY **183**

LIST OF FIGURES

4.1 Simple commodity production
4.2 Cumulative commodity production
4.3 Chains of performance
4.4 Combined performances
5.1 Aspirations, predictions and evaluation
10.1 Visual elements representation legend
10.2 Agent A publishes stake exchange offer to the network, promising 500B for 900A
10.3 The network matches A's stake exchange offer
10.4 Agent A holds 500B and the network holds 900A
10.5 An agent makes the network an (issuing credit) offer to exchange commodity X for liquidity tokens
10.6 Network matches the offer, accepting liquidity tokens from agent
10.7 Network gives credit to the agent who now holds a liquidity token liability and a commodity token asset
10.8 Agent receives a (clearing) offer from the network to exchange liquidity tokens for a commodity token
10.9 Agent matches credit (clearing) offer
10.10 Agent's credit liabilities are cleared through netting, so the network now holds a net asset of 30 liquidity tokens
10.11 Agent publishes a commodity exchange offer
10.12 Network matches commodity exchange offer
10.13 Agent now has commodity X and network commodity Y assets
10.14 Cross-token exchanges
11.1 Circuits of the new economic space

ACKNOWLEDGMENT

This book is the product of joint research, discovery and iteration since we began the Economic Space Agency (ECSA) project in 2015. Its composing process has consisted of diverse intellectual inputs, revelations, impasses, often heated debate and constantly-evolving analysis. It is not easy to step into the new economic space, where we constantly find ourselves in uncertain terrain. We've found out it is possible only by experimenting and risking together.

Many people and insights have been a part of this process; simply too many to mention here. The three of us who have authored this book see ourselves as bearers of the influences and express our deep appreciation of all engagement. There are some people who we wish to name whose intellectual input and cooperation has been vital and is directly recognizable in this book: Jonathan Beller, Fabian Bruder, Pekko Koskinen, Ben Lee, Joel Mason and Bob Meister. #livinginthespread #ECSAforever

We thank Matt Slater for producing an audio version of two drafts of this manuscript, Pablo Somonte Ruano for designing the cover and the figures and Stevphen Shukaitis, editor of Minor Compositions, for boldly taking on our manuscript.

We'd also like to thank our families and close friends for risking with us.

FOREWORD

ON ECONOMIC INTELLIGENCE

Jonathan Beller

Protocols for Postcapitalist Expression, written by ECSA (Economic Space Agency) thinkers Dick Bryan, Jorge López and Akseli Virtanen, marks an advance in the struggle for economic justice by directly addressing, and endeavoring to redress, the expropriation of the general intellect. The questions: Will the accumulated know-how of the species, alienated and, as Franco 'Bifo' Berardi (2012) put it, 'looking for a body,' lead to so-called humanity's absolute demise (along with massive unrest and incalculable ecosystemic damage)? Or, is there emerging a path towards reparations, restoration, a just economy, and thus, a sustainable planetary society? It is as if the political slogan 'No justice, no peace!' now defines the spread of the possible futures for the global timeline.

Significantly, *Protocols for Postcapitalist Expression* does not give up on economic calculation or computing. It acknowledges that Economic Intelligence exists in historically sedimented economic categories and practices, but at the same time it recognizes that the form of knowledge that existing accounting creates simply cannot care about, and much less *for*, everyone. Composing a virtual computer, capitalist accounting processes allow for the judicious, that is profitable, apportioning of resources by producing a matrix of the fluctuating costs of production. Capital accumulation may be optimized by watching, in Hayek's famous phrase, 'the hands of a few dials.' However, this calculus remains an imperial project beholden to the myriad violences of racial capitalism. In order to operationalize the world, the integration of money and computing reconstitutes the world as numbers, which is to say, as information. Arguably, we could even say, information is itself a derivative of the value-form.[1]

---

1   Information has emerged dialectically as the most general form for the products of capitalism defined as having both use-value and exchange value. Because of its abstract character, it is often forgotten that information must have a material substrate, be it the standard commodity or an array of atoms on a computer chip. For the briefest of sketches, consider that the commodity was always composed of readable material dif-

We might be forgiven for asking: does the collapse of values to exchange value, and more generally of qualities to number and thus to information have any liberatory potential whatsoever?

Postcapitalist Futures

Those who make it to the end of the TV series Westworld (Season 4), may discover where all this derivation and calculation may now be leading. Computing represents an arbitrage on intelligence that ultimately cheapens and thus discounts life. The show's verisimilitude, what we could think of as its late capitalist realism, serves as a kind of trailer for, or preamble to, what would appear – *is appearing* – as a mutation in global consciousness and capacity, due to the financialization of knowledge. Because computing is inexorably entwined with existing markets and the statistical and predictive strategies necessary for the optimization of returns, computing, in the show at least, takes over species-being as it rapidly becomes the species-grave. The only 'creature' who will be left to remember whatever beauty, alternative values, grace and capacity for love that may have been expressed in the centuries of human emergence, is an AI.

'One last dangerous game,' says Dolores to herself in the emptied world at the smoking end of four seasons of Westworld tragedies. What is that game? The series does not tell us, but the book before you might. Despite the real bleakness of the current world, we might propose, (and I think, must assume) that, here and now, some parts or fractions of 'us' have thus far survived the rapacious calculus of profit, and are actively seeking ways to do things otherwise. At the very least, we know that some 'we' or some parts of 'us' must now intervene if further catastrophes are to be prevented.

Through the lens of economics and financial calculus, *Protocols for Postcapitalist Expression* proposes a new form of economic intelligence and value-computing. The text proposes measures that do not collapse the qualitative concerns for well-being and being-with of those who cur-

---

ferences, differences in matter created through labor. As a wager to get from M to M,' the commodity's market legibility as a significant state of informed matter (a 'hieroglyph') has become increasingly computational. For my take on the networked commodity and the intimate connections between computing and capital see Beller (2017 and 2021). In each text I develop the argument that the general formula for capital can be rewritten M-I-M,' where M is money and I is information: Information replaces the commodity 'C' in Marx's classic formulation M-C-M.'

rently are subjects of and subject to racial capitalism. ECSA has sought a way to allow for the expression and persistence of qualitative values on a computational substrate, an economic medium, such that these values are capable of (collectively) organizing economy. In theory, it becomes possible to avoid the collapse of people's various pursuits into the value-form that is accumulated by capital and institutionalized through oppression, and to denominate quantities in terms of socially agreed upon qualities or qualifications, which is to say, values. Precluding the collapse of values by money and information opens a path to avoiding the collapse of space, time, and species existence by computational capitalism.

This proposed re-organization of value production and thus also of sociality requires a re-casting of what we today think of as the real or natural economic forms indexed under notions including 'equity,' 'credit' and (productive) 'labor.' Analytically in *Protocols*, these traditional terms have been decomposed, grasped as social arrangements and 'network effects,' and recomposed such that new conceptualizations and new types of actions and inflections – new socialities – become possible, while undervalued and marginalized traditional forms of sociality might thrive. Through this process of deconstruction and recomposition of actual and social computing, the text announces a possible socio-economic, computational strategy; a 'play,' for economics and for futurity, in what may well be the 'one last dangerous game.'

I say dangerous not only to refer to the current conditions on planet Earth, but because *Protocols* does accept aspects of the power of the value form and of economic calculus to organize societies at scale. Even as it recognizes the necessity for constellations of qualified local inputs that can persist on an economic substrate, it accepts the need for large scale organization, economic interoperability and network-specific units of account. It actually proposes that 'economy' needs to become more granular and more generalized. What needs to be altered is *what* the controls are, *who* has access to them, and the kind of literacy and feedback they require.

While *Protocols* is a book of politico-economic analysis and insight, it should also be read as a script for the means to reappropriate the general intellect and thus use collective knowledge for the good of the social and ecological body. Surfaced from the unconscious operating systems of capital and reformatted, the protocols for constituting and holding equity become those for the distributed sharing of stake and thus for collectivizing risks and returns. The protocols for bank credit and monetary issuance become protocols for the peer-to-peer issuance of credit and for peer-to-peer credit clearing that is interoperable through a network of peers. The protocols for the organization of labor become protocols for the distributed assemblage of 'performances.' Units of account become qualified measures and indices, devoted to the emergence of interoperable qualitative values. Economy moves from stranger-based to interpersonal to collective; the imperial organization of commodities by the accumulation of capital becomes the collection organization of sociality by all.

By shifting the architecture of economy and opening it as a design space, *Protocols* would enable, in principle, everyone to engage newly with and access differently what is, in effect, the historical objectifications of 'human' thought and practice endemic to capitalist infrastructure. But we could do so at a lower cost – to ourselves and to the lives of most of us! – and thereby, slowly, reclaim the wealth of our species capacities. Modifying accounting methods can create possibilities for the shedding of inequalities sedimented into capital. Users of the protocols, finding economic alternatives in one another, may refuse value extraction, get more of what we value for less, and be able to do so without exploiting others or being exploited. Altering the computing that backgrounds our sociality, *Protocols* would create zones of just and convivial social production (cooperatives, ephemeral and enduring) attuned to the values of like-minded co-creators cooperating in forms of mutual aid expressive of their shared values and concerns. The result of the use of qualitative values to account for and to organize economy at once produces and requires *a redesigned economic medium*, and *a new type of economic grammar* which utilizes different rules of composition, expression and accountability.

The text is the first complete edition of this new, if still rudimentary, economic grammar; it is a kind of manual for reprogramming the economic operating system. It is also a boot-strapping strategy to take back species abilities and creations that have been captured as assets (private property and monetary instruments). These assets include machinic fixed capital (platforms, code and clouds) as well as our own collateralized futures. The text, as an offer, is designed to open a spread between capitalist and postcapitalist futures. It would allow us to wager on the option that is justice (Meister).

Whether as software, as clouds or as platforms, capital owns and rents back to us the accumulated products of human minds – our know-how and knowledge. Resituating the abstractions of economic know-how, the ECSA Economic Space Protocol described by Bryan, Lopez and Virtanen, opens the possibility for creative capacities that are unalienated from their creators, that indeed produce a commonly-held set of capacities, a 'synthetic commons', particularized and directed by the living concerns of those who create it. It holds out the possibility that we might cooperate in new ways and use our performative powers to wager and indeed *finance* postcapitalist futures.

Economic media, redesigned, opens a spread on the social contract

Consider 'social media' – what can be clearly seen as a world-changing extractive technology grafted onto the sociality it at once enables and overdetermines. It is no secret that the mega-media platforms and their hardware make money while they make us sick. In this 21st century recasting and expropriation of the general intellect, now giving rise to financialized AI, social media platforms absorb communication and consciousness along with all of our struggles for meaning, pleasure, connection, fulfillment and liberation. Their interfaces, algorithms and data-bases convert our all-too-human aspirations into private property and thus into capital. Thus, the expression of our struggles for happiness, knowledge and communion with one another produce an alienated and therefore alienating wealth for others. All those desires for liberation end up producing their antithesis: capital. By turning our meanings into accumulated data that function for capital as contingent claims on value that we will produce in the future, the economic logic of social media turns any and all politics expressed by means of its platforms, including the politics of solidarity, love and living otherwise, into a practical politics of hierarchy and capitalist extraction. By converting all of our semiotic signals into financialized information, and thus into profits, 'social' media stripmines our libido, our consciousness, our imagination. In doing so, all the points of meaning and affect distributed across the socius and absorbed in one way or another by computing can thereby be grasped for performing social and organizational functions in a matrix of financialized information. This information in its architecture and management – *its organizational protocols* – transfers value up the stack, only to devalue the increasingly abject denizens of planet Earth. In the current world operating system, for which social media forms only one, albeit *paradigmatic*, layer of calculation, the meanings we create and the emotions we experience, however real and 'immediate' they may be, are interfaces with computing; they are productive interfaces with racial capitalism. As we perform, in the very expression of our quests for life, what elsewhere I have called 'informatic labor,' we experience first hand the alienation of our performative powers in the actually existing economic media of racial capitalism, that is, computational racial capitalism.

It is in this context of the latest stage of capitalism that something really interesting can finally be said about the rise of blockchain and cryptocurrency. This cryptographic medium, which has the network architecture of a messaging system, is a medium in the strong sense, akin, as I have elsewhere remarked, to photography in the mid-1800s or cinema in the early 1900s. Without turning any of the apparent key players here – the Satoshis and Vitaliks – into heroes, we might see in the 'mankind sets forth only such problems as he can solve [sic.]' scenario of history, a significant emergence in response to a collective demand. This emergence answers the call for a new form of *economic media* in order to express an alternate vision of the world. That expression, at first apparently as a monetary medium, begins to overturn the seemingly stable notions of asset, money, credit, labor, capital, derivative and many other 'known' financial entities implicit in, and indeed part of, the protocols of existing monetary media. The alternative vision is a programmable substrate that opens computational media to the possibility of a (re-)programming of the economic layer of computing by non-state and non-corporate actors. If we want to put a point on it, the great disruption underfoot is that *economy becomes programmable from below*. That, in itself, is a change in the semantics, as well as the capacities, of economy. When we recognize that our communications media are overdetermined in their function by existing monetary media, to the extent that they serve as an extension of its profit seeking logics, we begin to see that our communications media are already economic media, even though their capabilities seemed to have developed in separate and even autonomous domains.

The internet promised to democratize expression by enabling publishing and indeed broadcasting from below; but nothing about the internet changed the basic economic architecture of capitalist extraction. Indeed, in decentralizing communications, the internet extended and granularized the centralizing logics and logistics of capitalism, pushing them deeper into expressivity, thought and affect. It captures mass expressivity and converts it into capital. This colonization of the imaginary and symbolic registers results in a financialized cybernetics of mind. For democratization to happen in a meaningful way, the systems of accounts inherent in many-to-many distributed media, be they networked monetary systems (USD) or communications (Facebook), must become programmable from below. For this to happen, platforms and computing must be made programmable from below. The cybernetics of economic media must be deleveraged from capital accumulation. This transformation, and how it may be achieved, is indicated in *Protocols*.

Why do the cybernetics of sociality matter? For our futurity and indeed for our survival, we require an alternative to monological systems of value as expressed in national monies. We require, in short, a *multi-dimensional* modality of valuation not bound by the econometrics and informatic collapse inherent in capital. Multidimensional valuation implies the creation of eco-social relations that can dialogically express and preserve discourse-based values on an economic substrate, while being programmable in real time by any and all participants. (Before anyone up and leaves at the sudden thought of having to wake up and program, think first of an interface like *Instagram* with a tunable economic logic built in. Think also of how these already-familiar technologies of social mediation change our experiences and actualities of relation and 'reality.') We require the power to qualify value and to allow such qualification to both persist in an economic system and be computable. Ultimately, we will require that this system itself be collectively owned; that it be a commons.

Robust economic media, capable of heteroglossic and dialogical forms of account, are required to create a multiperspectival values-system. These media demand far more than merely a non-national variant of monetary media expressive of the capitalist value form. While the non-national dimension of cryptocurrencies introduced a significant rupture with conventional monetary substrates, platformed as they are as national currencies on nation states, their legally recognized institutions and their military police, this ultimately simple replatforming of singular denominations on distributed computing by existing cryptocurrencies is not enough. Bitcoin did in fact break the nationally managed monopolies on 21st century monetary issuance by introducing a scalable currency(/asset/option) platformed on distributed computing, but it has done, and can do, little or nothing to challenge the monologic denomination of value as a one-dimensional, that is as a unitary, currency format. Bitcoin may contest the nation, but it, and its fetishism, is all about it being an option on the value-form as historically worked up under, and as, capitalism. The question 'Bitcoin or USD' scarcely touches the relations of production. We must see clearly that the 'disintermediation' of 'trusted third parties' and of existing states, even if it were to be accomplished, is only one part of the picture of a liberated monetary medium, which is also to say, a liberated socius. We require the possibility for *anyone* to offer denominations of value that can be taken up by those who share such values as specified and indeed offered in the proffered denomination. Only then will we have a genuinely multiperspectival system.

To foreground this possibility of reprogramming a global operating system, one that is at once computational and financial, stakes a claim for a different order of significance for cryptomedia. Even Ethereum, and other 'Layer 1' projects that utilize smart contracts and allow for further token issuance, lack a robust grammar for composable asset creation and peer-to-peer issuance; a grammar that would allow for the on-chain preservation of qualities and the spontaneous creation of denominations. Outlining the emergence of a far more robust economic medium than what is currently wet dreamt by the 'when Lambo?' crypto bros going on about libertarian forms of self-sovereignty, *Protocols* posits a transformation not just of economy but of sociality, of subjectivity, of national politics and of ecopolitics by means of the composition and recomposition of relations of production. For those actively working in the ECSA project, what unites us as current contributors, even among our many differences, is that the radical development of economic media means that the intelligence of sociality, including that which has not been subsumed, can work for the socius, rather than be captured, farmed, privatized and put back on the market in an arbitrage on knowledge, where proprietary innovation captures the returns.

As *Protocols* explains, robust economic media mean that, through the equitable nomination of new asset classes and the collective denomination of values (practices which will require networked recognition, participation and validation), innovation can be collectively shared rather than capitalized. The text argues that through the sharing of stake, wealth, whose actual origins are inexorably social, can be socialized. We might add that *Protocols* intimates that society might ultimately be decolonized because it would, after a time, no longer be organized from the imperial standpoint of Value. The deep plurality of being, though suppressed in commodity reification and egoism alike, but in fact constituting each and all, might at last be felt and actualized. It means, in short, that the other person might at last become not a limit to your freedom, but the realization of it.

Note that no other major crypto project addresses the world in these terms. Nor do they think very deeply, if at all, about the adjoined problem of sovereignty *and* subjectivity, or the cybernetics thereof. It has become clearer to the participants in the ECSA project that the form many recognize as the sovereign individual is but an iteration of the value form, an avatar of capital.[2] But given these economic and formal overdeterminations of agency and the reign of this type of sovereignty, we see that history, or at least collective survival, demands better chances. We have had enough of egomania and nationalism. The significance of things on the ground must be registered and economically expressed. To those ends, *Protocols for Postcapitalist Expression* is in pursuit of something of a different order; something that must *risk* the increasing granularization and resolution of computing and of the economy that computing has always expressed. *Protocols* must risk this granularization and resolution *because that is what is already happening*. But collective survival necessitates something that also simultaneously enables a *detournement* of extant economic logics and practices. ECSA's analysis recognizes that the concentration of agency, whether in the form of the propertied individual or of the propertied immortal individuals called corporations and states, requires the collapse of the concerns of others, of their perspectives and of their information. It is precisely the refusal of that collapse that motivates the work presented in *Protocols*.

The book reveals another economic path than to have your interests collapsed as bank interest. The world is / we are ready for an economic and computational grammar that is answerable in new ways. That also means programmable in new ways, where programming by the many becomes both the way to answer economic precarity and the means to posit and preserve a plurality of qualitative values. We will answer economy with economy! The leveraged monologue of national monies, the leveraged computing architectures of privately-owned platforms, the near monopoly on who can issue what kinds of monies and types of financial instruments, including derivatives, must, if the people and ecosystems of Earth are to thrive, be delimited and, in their current forms, swept away. All of these media, we now perceive, are not only financial forms, but also informatic forms: programs in every sense of the word. They are integrated, interoperating systems, and are systems of account beholden, ultimately, to little other than profit in nationally-denominated monies;

---

2   Whatever its specific embodiment, the sovereign subject that dominates Western philosophy is the subject of property. 'He' is semiotically, psychologically ideologically, and materially constituted through 'his' whiteness and cis-masculinity, the outputs of the representational and material systems that are among his dividends from colonization and slavery.

monies, we can remind ourselves, that are optimized by states and supported by their historical, institutionalized forms of organizational inequality, prisons and warlike foreign policy.

ECSA understands these systems of account, whether conceived of as interfaces, databases, financial instruments and ledgers, or as forms of money or money as capital, to be *semantic forms*; forms that have meaning and thus compatibility and commensurability with one another, but also, and as importantly, forms that put exorbitant pressure on life and its meanings. Today's socio-economic systems threaten insolvency, war and extinction. They threaten all forms of meaning-making that are close to the flesh and close to the earth: desire, the imagination, consciousness, speech, writing, landscape, oceans, the body, the self. They pressure meaning, living and life, and can do so because money is composed of a set of contracts; contracts that, in effect, have subsumed, and then become, the social contract. That subsumption of the social contract by the protocols of the media of racial capitalism is the ultimate meaning of 'the dissolution of traditional societies.' The ECSA project, to create non-extractive, disalienating, just economy and sociality, is given new impetus with this volume and the promise it holds. A recasting of the current social contract has long been dreamt. At last, perhaps, we have an option on postcapitalism; one that, by reimagining the who and the how in the creation of contracts, will allow us to open and live in the spread between two basic futures: collectivism or extinction.

The 'one last dangerous game' proposed here feels correct and indeed compelling. It contends that, against disaster, our species has some chance of survival where the odds increase if we can use collective intelligence to wager livable futures. Whether in the form of decolonial resurgence, platform cooperatives, or hospice, I cannot say, but to offer the care the planet requires seems to involve an even deeper entry of the species and the bios into informatics and economics. It will not be lost on anyone that the digital operations of these very things have already done so much harm.

The book in your hands or on your screen would be a new beginning. It represents not a settling of accounts but a new mode of accounting and of being accountable to one another. A revaluation of values becomes possible by means of what is here called an 'economic grammar,' a grammar for the assemblage of new relations of production and thus new modes of production, and new forms of (collective) relation and self-governance. The core idea is to express values differently, such that the qualitative concerns of any and potentially all members of society may be expressed at once semantically and economically on a persistent and programmable substrate. These values may be assembled by many parties and then used to coordinate performances in accord with socially agreed upon and thus collectively mandated metrics. 'Agreement' here is a semantic and an economic term that, though formally accurate, is not quite adequate to affectively express the character and indeed the *feel* of social co-creation ECSA sees as becoming possible with a new grammar for the multitudes.

As a starting point among starting points, this text comes out of years of research at ECSA and offers the most comprehensive treatment and latest refinements of a set of protocols based on an analysis of finance, monetary networks, and the extractive processes of postmodern value production. A critique of this latter, namely the capture of semiotic and other forms of social performances by ambient computing, has enabled ECSA to endeavor to liberate social performances from such capture. 'Performance' in this text has emerged, dialectically as it were, as the most general act of production; what is extracted on the job, at work, on social media, in maker-spaces and in the arts. Always dialogical, performance can be taken as a category of social interaction and world-creation that names the emergent superset for other productive capacities designated by terms including labor, attention, attention economy, cognition, cognitive capitalism and virtuosity.

Counter-intuitively perhaps, the strategy includes the generalization of the power to issue – to issue financial instruments that not only fund co-creation, but create possibilities for speculation and arbitrage. A capacity to express, issue, and wager on shared futures shifts the economic ground, particularly for the smallest players who currently have no access to scripting economic protocols with which a shared future might be wagered. Can we create with and for one another's todays and tomorrows in ways that cause less suffering and are more convivial than they could be were we to attempt to do it in the capitalist markets? Can we use our powers of co-creation to siphon value out of the capitalist system in order to build a collectivist postcapitalism? To be dramatic, part of the political answer to the obscene leverage of class power and national power on the masses, is to generalize, which is to say democratize, the power to write (co-author) derivative contracts (co-author since in these protocols, all issuance is bilateral). It is time that the masses leveraged our claims, by creating our own economic networks with a new grammar and co-created, optional rules of play. This power, made possible by platforming protocols for cooperation around values creation, allows for an extended practice of community as well as the elaboration of what Randy Martin (2013a, 2015; Lee and Martin 2016) called 'social derivatives.' The social derivative is a cultural instrument that is wagered in social spaces already shot through with financial volatility. It allows marginalized groups, in Martin's words, to 'risk together to get more of what we want.' It is in this way that the logic contained in *Protocols*, that allows for the mass authorship of social derivatives, may well succeed in democratization where the internet failed.

While this power for anyone to write a derivative may sound esoteric (or even impossible and/or undesirable) – and part of the book that follows this foreword *is* somewhat esoteric – a breaking down the barriers to the publishing of derivative instruments means that, in a world already rendered precarious by the history of racial capitalism, everyone (not just elites) may be better able to manage their undeniable risk by organizing their economy, cooperatively and collectively, and in terms of what is valuable to them. If neoliberalism taught us anything, it is that the way out of the problems of capitalism cannot, and will never, be through the creation of more capitalism. That is why we have reimagined the cryptotoken as a set of programmable capabilities (agreements) that may be enabled only when recognized and thereby validated by peers. Their semantic content represents a wager that the relationship, or agreement, they formalize expresses something of value (anything whatever) to both parties. Because each party or agent is enabled in the network through composing themselves – by entering into a portfolio of such tokenized arrangements that are in principle limitless – the wealth of each agent then becomes a composite of the qualified interests of others.

The Revaluation of Value

A social derivative is a wager in the cultural sphere that responds to volatility in order that a local group can 'risk together.' *Protocols* has tried to formalize a way to express those socio-economic wagers, such that others can validate or join them non-extractively by means of their own staking and/or performance. It becomes possible, at first in principle but later practically, to nominate and denominate values and then to collectively organize socio-economic outcomes of any type that preserve, foster and realize said values: differentiable, negotiable and socially agreed upon qualitative values. This is economic expressivity. When many actors are offering such semio-economic proposals and performances on a collectively-owned economic media platform, socio-economic actors such as ourselves may engage in a multidimensional system of valuation and production attuned to anything whatever: clean beaches, dance cultures, reforestation, spoken word, prison abolition, decolonial resurgence, blood free computing, and much more. When we have a way of sharing risk, both by sharing stake (staking a performance) and/or offering performance, in a variety of qualitative outcomes by means of a scalable peer-to-peer network, we get forms of distributed risk and reward that can create a distributed form of awareness – a consciousness attuned to the specific interests of many others. This awareness results from, and constitutes, a new form of economic space and new form of economic agency: economic space agency. It will also transform subjectivity/objectivity and the membrane between self and other.

Though this new economic language may sound like it requires a learning curve too steep for the 'average' person, the literacy and innovation will come, just as it did and does on paradigm shifting platforms such as Facebook, Instagram and TikTok. Here, the emerging paradigm comes with the social programmability inherent in expressivity directly linked to the programmability of economy. The postcapitalist economy will be about creating new forms of social relations; new relations of production that are qualitative and non-extractive. Collectively, we will script parameters that express our semantically based, qualitative values, and collectively we will manifest these values. We may hope, and perhaps expect, that within a few years or decades, folks will not be programming their fractal celebrity; they will be programming together the nuanced worlds they actually want to live in and creating the relationships they want to have there.

There is much to learn, and much to be skeptical of. To answer the global challenges set forth by history will require the input and discernment of millions if not billions of people – it is not a technocratic endeavor. Already there are millions among us who feel the need for alternative economic forms and for a type of radical economy and/or finance that answers on-the-ground problems of access to liquidity. The movement towards basic income is just one expression of this desire. In *Protocols* what becomes possible is *basic equity* founded upon ones' social relations. Our requirement for emancipation is not further dispossession of others or ourselves but expanded access to the social product, particularly for those who do not have it. We agree with the growing mass need for our desires and our capacities to count and be counted in ways that remand the benefits to those who sustain the world and remake it everyday.

It is not lost on us that, in the current economic calculus, a tree, an individual and even a people can be worth more dead than alive, more incarcerated or encamped then free – and we hardly need to mention deforestation, police killings, settler colonialism and genocide to make the point here. But this book, though still incomplete in significant ways and offering more of a possible way forward than any as yet definitive answer, offers what approaches a concrete plan; one that may move readers from increased eco-social literacy to active participation in building an alternative economy. It would organize social participation that will create greater literacy and expressivity even as it endeavors to collectively create and thus instantiate, a new economic medium–an economic medium for the expression and collective management of a postcapitalist economy; a medium that is socially and ecologically responsive, which is to say, increasingly non-extractive because its interfaces are made to be just. The entire project stands or falls on this wager. However, that said, the book is but a seed, one that only collective uptake, and with it collective revision, can nurture and grow.

Lastly, the desire for non-, ante-, anti- and/or post-capitalism is in no way an invention of this text; what feels new here is the method. I would say that it proposes a new way to mobilize what Harney and Moten (2013) call the general antagonism, and with it, a new form of revolution. What would it be? A *detournement* of financial processes and tools, a slow takeover of the economic operating system occupying planet earth by those whose interests have been collapsed into bank interest. Indeed, it is the *incapacity* to do just this granular and collective reformatting of the economy that has marked the failure of previous revolutions. Thus far, beyond the initial desperation, beauty and romanticism of revolutionary movements, we have mostly had various efforts at a seizing of the state that result in the reintroduction and replication of the gendered, racial and hierarchical logics of capitalism. From the Soviets, to the PRC, to scores of post-colonial states, we are familiar with the outcomes. The limitations were both of imagination and technology; movements weighed down by default notions of centralization and bureaucratic organization, notions that informed both emergent states and the discrete state computing that would develop to run them and all the others. This time, with another century of struggle and know-how, if we all listen to history and to the claims of the denizens of Earth, things may be different.

The ECSA project opens a spread on racial capitalism and endeavors to use its historically consolidated capacities (*our* capacities), including the power of financial instruments and computing, to wager on postcapitalist outcomes. Contrary to racial capitalism, the arbitrage on intelligence proposed here is to reduce the cost to the planet for collective re-imagination and re-organization, while also collectivizing the returns on the benefits of creating more convivial forms of life. We will reduce the price of survival, in terms of violence to others, in terms of the individual requirements for the value-form (money), and in absolute terms. Perhaps we will collectivize values creation and distribution/sharing to the point of overcoming the value form of capital itself. In any case, by utilizing the accumulated knowledge implicit in financial instruments and computing derived from, but not beholden to, capitalism, we will be creating a grammar for postcapitalist economic expression. The ECSA vision might just open an option on postcapitalist futures. This option would be one where we can risk together for non-capitalist outcomes, and do so from within capital. As Jodi Melamed (2015:82) says:

> Marx finds value itself to be a pharmekon: it is a poison because it is a measure of how much human labor has been estranged and commodified by capital, yet it is also a medicine because it provides a way to grasp individual human efforts as alienated social forces, which revolutionary struggles can turn toward collective ends.

Let's do that.

CHAPTER 1

INTRODUCTION

1.1 Contesting the current order

Despite a deepening climate disaster, consecutive global economic crises and a socially devastating pandemic, the last two decades have found us living in an era of capitalist triumphalism. In almost all capitalist countries, political leaders celebrate their achievements in promoting economic growth and stock market record highs while 'successfully managing' wage growth. State 'reforms' of all kinds have seen growing precarity of those whose living standard is low and growing wealth and security for those at the top. Indeed increasing inequality seems to be the current engine of economic growth and it is only in the very recent past that concerns for the biosphere have looked like a constraint on that momentum.

At an individual level, it is now clear to many people that the economic aspirations of a previous generation are no longer available to the majority of the population, and especially younger people. The combination of education, finding permanent employment, and saving diligently in a bank or pension fund is no longer a formula for life security – it's not available and increasingly it's not aspired to. Education is now about debt accumulation with no guarantee it will generate the capacity for repayment; permanent employment and the idea of a predictable, secure income is, for a growing proportion of the working population, both unavailable and oppressive, and saving in banks sees negative real returns while wage payments into pension funds constrain current living standards in the name of a self-reliant old age.

The starkest challenges to capitalist triumphalism have not come from what we would call the traditional 'left': the trades union or the socialist organizations. Predominantly, they have been in defensive mode, trying to hold back change. The emerging challenge is from a different source: people who simply don't want to play by the rules of capitalist economics; who want to define themselves outside its discipline and its system or rewards.

Generally, these people aren't in trades union or political parties; they may not see themselves as being on the 'left.' So how do we profile these people? Perhaps they are open source developers, but their designs can't be easily monetized, or won't be funded by the internet monopolies. They may well create social benefits, but their innovation doesn't comply with corporate business plans. Perhaps they see themselves as a custodian of the commons, but can't see a way to expand the organization of that role to the scale required. Or maybe they care passionately about environmental decay and work to build biosustainability. But they know that, for all the official posturing about sustainability and concessions to green industry, the current system will never pursue deep changes that will save the planet, because returns to investors will always shout loudest in any debate. They might work in various forms of human care, for low or even zero income, and generally without much social recognition, but they know their contribution is socially essential and should be rewarded with a reasonable income. Or perhaps they work in art and design, and hear governments pronounce on the importance of cultural creation, but see them deliver miniscule funding to people who are indeed performing critical social roles.

What all these endeavors have in common is that they generate social benefits but aren't recognized as profitable in a capitalist sense; indeed as not creating a surplus, to use a more general term. In a Covid-dominated world, with state fiscal austerity and protracted economic downturn awaiting, their financial future is bleak. Will audiences return with spending power; will governments still give grants; will philanthropists feel as generous?

An alternative for these sorts of people could be to participate in an economy that values differently: both in the sense of different modes of calculating economic 'value' and with different collective social and ethical values. This would be an economy not driven specifically by profitability, nor reliant on state subsidies or philanthropy, but one which draws on aspirations and affects, to value social, creative and environmental benefits, without reducing all contributions into a price. Artists and designers, along with people performing care roles – care for people or for the environment – could be rewarded for what they actually contribute to society.

This is the economy that we are aspiring to see built. We are pitching our network design particularly to the generation of people who want to do it differently: who know from personal experience that the conventional economic system is not serving them well individually or collectively, and are looking for ways to participate in building a collective future of their shared design.

Our proposal is that analysis must start at the frontier of current change, and work out how to subvert its momentum. A critical factor in framing this direction is the recognition that social and economic power has shifted dramatically since the 1970s from industrial capital, and the workplace-based unions who battled it, to finance, where there is little organized resistance; at least not the old kind of resistance. Finance is too elusive, too liquid and mobile to be trapped in power battles with organized labor, and the people employed by finance are not generally in a union-based labor force.

Economically and politically, if we want to build postcapitalism, we must start by recognising this power of finance and challenge it by building a different finance. The ultimate goal is an economy of production, animated by alternative social and ethical values, and the starting point is finance.[1]

Finance is both dynamic and fragile. In its current dominant form, it goes to where the profits are greatest, but it instantly retreats when the profits are not appearing. So it is a direct discipline on those who need finance: they must deliver profits, or they suffocate.

But its liquidity and mobility is also its vulnerability, for finance depends critically on the state to provide it with a money instrument and to underwrite its social reputation and its profit. The US-initiated subprime crisis of 2007-2008 and, even more emphatically, the 2020s Covid pandemic have revealed how the fast and free movement of finance can undermine its own conditions of existence. In both periods we have seen nation states (predominantly through their central banks) having to throw money at financial markets to secure liquidity and sustain financial market profits. In 2008, the US Federal Reserve Chairman argued behind closed doors that the state has to do whatever it takes to preserve financial market profits or economic disaster would follow.[2] By 2020, the

---

[1] Inspirational Marxist historian Eric Hobsbawm (1978) contended that the 1970s must be read as a crisis for working class organizations; a crisis from which they have not recovered. Our response is that collective endeavors that move beyond the control of capital must be focussed at the frontier of capitalist development – financial innovation – not in nostalgia for a resurgent industrial proletariat.

[2] 'If we don't do this, we may not have an economy on Monday' is a statement attributed to Federal Reserve Chairman, Ben Bernanke, in a meeting on Thursday September 18, 2008

financial institutions were themselves confidently asserting the demand for the state to guarantee their profitability.³

Somehow, we have collectively fallen into the position where these institutions hold the key to our viability. The oppression of the treadmill of working for wages and the intrusion of the logic of finance into daily life now express both the triumph of capitalism and the reason so many people are resisting its consequences.

But if the current era is about the shift from the power of industrial capital to the power of financial capital, then the new, emerging forms of opposition need to be uniting around finance. Some have been tried, but ultimately they succumb to the power of what they oppose. In 2011 *Occupy Wall Street* was the initial instantiation of this opposition in its contemporary form, but it was conceived as a protest and a spatial obstacle in the movement of financial actors; not an alternative finance. Occupy could be dispersed by the state power of the police. In 2021, social media mobilized a crash of hedge funds short-selling GameStop (GME) shares, and with short-term success, but ultimately at significant cost to participants. Neither was sustainable.

The idea that there could be a different finance, or that certain monetary roles could be performed outside the current financial system and without state backing, had already emerged in 2008, but not initially in a recognizable form. That new possibility came into being with Satoshi Nakomoto's *Bitcoin White Paper* (2008). Its implications have become worrying for states and big financial institutions alike, for it usurps their power to determine the rules of finance and how the economy should operate.

This is where the domain of cryptographically enabled decentralized economic-organizational systems (a.k.a cryptotokens) opens the possibility of a challenge to capitalist triumphalism in a way that the old industrial-based organizations of the left now cannot and probably never could:

---

with Treasury Secretary Henry Paulson and House Speaker Nancy Pelosi, in his advocacy of a $700 billion bailout plan for banks. https://www.nytimes.com/2008/10/02/business/02crisis.html

3   Financial institutions in the period 2020-2022 might be depicted as financial terrorists, with sticks of illiquidity strapped to their chests, threatening to blow themselves up, and taking the rest of us with them, unless the state guaranteed market liquidity. And states gave those terrorists exactly what they wanted. The terrorist ransom payment is better known as Quantitative Easing, and because of it, the balance sheet of the Federal Reserve (to reference just one index) reached $8.9 trillion by mid 2022, up from $0.9 trillion in 2007, $2.3 trillion in December 2008, and $4.2 trillion in February 2020.

it challenges the state's and financial institutions' monopoly over finance.

This challenge means taking finance outside the state and the current financial institutions. We propose networks of people, with their own financial capacities – units of account, distributed credit issuance and ways of investing, measuring and rewarding – building a collective alternative to capitalism in a way that the traditional left no longer can.

That's still not how most people are thinking of crypto, although attitudes are changing rapidly. One widespread image, especially from those invested in the current financial status quo, is of cryptotokens as scams and crypto markets as casinos of speculative bets. An alternative image is of a libertarian anti-statism of freely associating individuals, pursuing their own goals in the name of some individualistic conception of 'freedom.' Both of these views warrant direct critique, and these will be developed in subsequent chapters. It will be revealed that they may not be 'wrong,' for there is evidence of all these characteristics, but the critiques are trivial and dangerous in equal measure. They are trivial because crypto token design keeps evolving and markets in aggregate seem resistant to the effects of scams and volatility (though some individuals certainly lose wealth). Continual predictions of the pending demise of the cryptocurrency markets are consistently wrong. The critiques are dangerous because they are premised on the idea that, with sufficient diatribe, crypto currencies and the technology they represent will simply disappear. So they encourage the perspective of crypto as a cult, and thereby discourage the importance of a wider population inquiring into the potential for new ways of thinking with cryptographically enabled technologies.

Beneath these ideologically-defined polemics, 'crypto' simply offers various versions of a technology of communication and exchange: the possibility of coordinating chains of interactions without a central 3rd party authority. And basically that's all it can do. Economic protocol design must be much more, but critically built on that game-changing technology. So our project is to push past this ideological polemic and immediately frame crypto technological innovation as a site of social contestation about the sorts of social interactions we are seeking to facilitate, built on top of a technology of communication and exchange.

Our project is to design a network where participants:

- *interact* in the creation of new outputs (not simply gamble on price movements);

- *communicate* in the determination of what is deemed value-creating (not driven by private appropriation of profit);
- *coordinate* the assemblage of production (not corporate);
- *bind* in the building of a commons (not individualistic); and
- *launch* the capacity to scale and reproduce in sustainable ways (not reliant on on-going injections of external funding).

We cannot, and should not, pre-determine the outputs that people produce, nor what constitutes value or the content of the commons. The people who have participated in building the Economic Space Protocol outlined in this document all have views about what sorts of outcomes we would personally like to see, but it is critical that these are not predetermined in protocol design, that distributed network interactions and not a central authority coordinates network development. That's why we frame our work as a political project as well as a project of network design.

1.2 What does the future hold?

Blockchain-based innovations for economic and financial design are evolving rapidly. Most recently, DAOs, DeFi, stablecoins, DEXs, liquidity farming, NTF markets and creator and community tokens offer expansive new possibilities. But what will be the next frontier; the next big development?

What does history suggest?

By today's standards, history moved in slow motion. It records that money, roughly as we now know it, dates from about the 7th century BCE. Recognizably modern banking developed in the Northern Italian coastal cities of Florence, Venice and Genoa in the 14th century, driven by the funding requirements of long-distance trade. This banking evolved over the next few centuries from funding commerce to funding the rise of industrial production, and a system we call capitalism. The formation of joint stock companies and a liquid stock exchange in the mid 19th century transformed ownership of capital to decentralized protocols, though the division between ownership and management served to re-centralize the control. This is the corporate capitalism we know today.

In cryptohistory, that long evolution looks like it is happening over little more than a decade. Bitcoin as a new, distinctive p2p form of money arrived in 2009, with DeFi (decentralized finance, or banking protocols) becoming prevalent a decade later; funding new kinds of distributed exchange and money games. Governance mechanisms of DAOs and in-house treasury functions, broadly replicating the roles of the corporate form, followed immediately afterwards. History would say that these developments must surely evolve to the funding of a new era of production as its next logical step. But that next step is yet to emerge, and its possible shape is still unclear.

It is already clear this future will be 'post-industrial,' with information at the center, as both its predominant input and output. But what will be its social shape; what technical capacities and social relations will it build upon? There are two complementary, contemporary developments that are critical: distributed money and the iteration of the internet that brings decentralization back into its heart; also known as Web3 or the Economic Web.

First, distributed money. The development of blockchain technology opened the possibility of re-thinking money: what it is, who issues it and who controls its value. Bitcoin initiated a new form of money, but it remains centrally issued and controlled by the global virtual agent that maintains the ledger in singular blockchain. Network protocol design creates the possibility for a *distributed* money system where there is no central money issuer. All agents can be issuers, while network-recognized collateral for such lending means the money system can nonetheless remain stable. These are already the foundations of current shadow banking. Such a money system is elaborated below.

Distributed 'money' can then be put at the service of pursuing post-capitalist economic values (modes of calculating), effectively superseding the profit-based calculus that is embedded in the price of and access to conventional money. In relation to capitalism, we can now have a parallel (but interacting) money system, associated with a parallel (but interacting) value system.

Second, Web3. We have designed an economy that draws on the data and network capacities that were driving the initial development of the internet more than forty years ago: *an internet native economic system*. We have built on the vision of Web3 and the re-imagined potential in the internet: its capacity for trust and verifiability, for scalability and decentralized relations, with users owning and in charge of their own data. The potential of Web3 opens a new economic imaginary, where peer-to-peer economic networking protocols can create performances and outputs out of information creation and exchange, distributed computation, connectivity and network relationships. Codified incentives and enforcement can motivate new economic relations, with informational value transmitted as tokens. There is a lot to absorb in these last sentences, and the process tagged here will be elaborated in the chapters below.

We see Web3 engaging the native potential of the internet, challenging and going beyond the power of the current major internet players (tech companies, financial institutions and other collectors and users of consumer data) who have channeled, and even prevented, the realization of this potential by means of copyright, paywalls, advertising, data extraction, etc. so that internet expansion remains consistent with tech company profitability.[4] A blockchain-based distributed money doesn't need to 'take on' these corporate giants; it is sufficient simply to sidestep them.

Web3 offers the potential for what we call 'economic media' for expressing economic-organizational relationships and networks. The capacities of distributed economic communication have yet to emerge. Bitcoin, for all its innovation, preserves fiat money's monologic monetary value ('price'), not the broad sweep of social meaning that can attach to exchange.[5] Other crypto designs (such as Ethereum) have attempted through smart contracts to make this expression on the blockchain more robust by creating programmable money, but the full development of a cohesive and expressive, decentralized medium of value networks has not yet been achieved. We are building on this aspiration.

When we turn to finance, we see the same processes that were just depicted in relation to the internet. Credit, which is essentially a system of IOUs, requires systemic trust, scale and collateral. The current world of institutional banking and finance performs these and other functions in a way that extracts wealth from, and imposes surveillance on, those who borrow and lend. Decentralized Finance (DeFi), like Web3, is offering the alternative to this corporate control by developing decentralized credit issuance and other financial products of risk management. But can DeFi develop the extra stage and link to the funding of investment in new systems of production? We believe that this requires an analytical leap:

---

4   Many people now make this argument. See, for example, Dixon (2018) and Buterin (2017)

5   From our perspective, bitcoin identified the trusted intermediary component of capitalism. That is, capitalism's regime of verification depends on trust which, in its turn, ultimately depends on states' monopoly on violence and coercion. Bitcoin expressed that there can be more dimensions of freedom. It opened the question of the sociality of value: it showed that value is always social, organizational and institutional. But bitcoin didn't give a language to express it. The Economic Space Protocol is a grammar for expressing the sociality of value.

to think of stake (ownership of investment) as the preferred collateral for reciprocal issuance of credit.[6] It will give credit a material and expandable foundation. Financing investment in new forms of production (performances) will itself open up new possibilities for DeFi that link to the 'real' economy.

For us, the goal of realizing the potential of Web3 for economic design, extending DeFi into investing and staking, and building an economic space of many collective values are all parts of the same vision. These connections are our depiction of collaborative finance (CoFi),[7] and the proposition that it is through finance that a network most actively coheres. But, in connection to our starting question of what the future holds, we need a clear stepping off point. In capitalism, it is the state that economically ties the present to the future[8] It issues treasury bonds and oversees the yield curve, it sets the base interest rates from which commercial rates follow and it manipulates exchange rates, etc.. But in a new economy, it can be the protocol designs of distributed finance that economically links the present to the future.[9] So it is critical that the interaction of credit, investment and exchange – all dimensions of CoFi – are integral to protocol design.

The subsequent chapters of this analysis work systematically through these issues, moving from the creation of new products (Chapter 4) to staking their creation and distributing their outputs (Chapter 5), to a system of credit that keeps the system of performances and distribution flowing (liquid) (Chapter 8).

---

6   The trend to use equities as collateral for loans is increasingly prevalent. In 2017 the US Securities and Exchange Commission reconsidered the rules which prevented institutional market participants from pledging and accepting equity as collateral in the US securities lending market. In March 2020 the US Federal reserve, looking to rebuild liquidity in the Covid pandemic, enabled banks to borrow cash against stocks and corporate bonds.

7   This term has been used in the 'sharing economy' literature for quite a few years. We use it here in a specifically blockchain-enabled way, as initially proposed by a local currency research team at *Informal Systems*. See, for example, https://cofi.informal.systems. See also Fleischman, et al (2020).

8   Antonio Negri (1968) was astute when, in 1968, he observed that connecting the present to the future in a capitalist economy is the responsibility of the state. In the absence of this state role, we see the need to make the link financially will potentially be made by futures and option contracts.

9   The argument here is crystalised in Chapter 8.5.

1.3 A new economic space; new economic performances

To conceive of a viable postcapitalism that gives focus to collective, shared futures, we start from the proposition that the economy is a network: a group of agents interacting under certain agreements, (i.e. protocols) which define the relations that form the network, and how its state may change.

Protocols involve design choices and they can embed the capacity to be redesigned at the will of the network itself. A postcapitalism must be built 'inside' capitalism and find its own way to emerge 'out of' capitalism.

Our approach combines the radical rupture of bitcoin with the integration of CoFi and adds to them the agenda of expressing different collectively-defined means of defining and measuring value, to build an open, new economic space. Building a whole economy represents a profound change in direction for cryptodesign. We call it the Economic Space Protocol.[10] The Economic Space Protocol is the language that network participants, through their agents,[11] use to interact, program and operate an economic space. These social and economic interactions are of the participants' own determination, but not in circumstances of their own choosing. It is important to highlight that the existence of the network and its protocols is the foundation of interactions between participants: they interact *through* the network.

But nor is the network imposed on participants. Although an agent ensures adherence to the protocol, when the protocols are designed the 'right' way, participants operate in an open and coordinated space where they can collectively assert sovereignty over the network; not via a central authority, but via distributed network governance. Choice is individual and sovereignty is collective. The objective of design is to enable a process of sovereignty that sees participant decisions incentivized to enhance shared goals. The effect would be to bring the collective and each participant into alignment.

Framed this way, the economy is a programmable, designable medium: not in a mechanistic, reductionist sense of guaranteed processes and outcomes, but in the sense that how the economy works and its key conventions – the kind of relations, interactions, agents, incentives and

---

[10] See López, J. 'Economic performance: The Economic Space Protocol.' http://economicperformance.manifold.one. See Appendix 1.1 for a brief summary of its current application.

[11] Agents are defined more precisely in Chapter 3.2. In this context, they can be thought of as individuals or self-organized groups of individuals under a singular network identity.

values the network operates under – can become simultaneously an automation space and a design space, continuously open to its participants.

We started this chapter with the contention that crypto developments have not yet given focus to new ways of producing, or what we prefer to call 'performances.'[12] Performances involve processes of new value creation. Understood more broadly than 'production,' performances can focus on issues of social meaning, shared risk taking, and affect. It is important, therefore, that our initial approach to the Economic Space Protocol centers on performances. The Economic Space Protocol sets out three critical features of performances:

> *New forms of economic participation.* Capitalism produces one form of incentives, one form of ownership, one money system and one stream of value.[13] The Economic Space Protocol enables a different stream of value, with different incentives, ownership and tokens. Agents in the network design their own performance expressions, including the internal relations of performing and the social outcomes they claim for their outputs.[14] These relations, as well as the outcomes of a performance will be evaluated by the network as contributions to the creation of new economic value. The network is not specifying exactly how 'postcapitalist production' should be organized, but when protocols are not designed around extractive class relations, the most suitable forms of performance relations are created by agents themselves.

---

12 The distinctive meaning of a 'performance,' and its deeper significance, is elaborated in Chapter 4.

13 Other forms of incentives, ownership and money do indeed exist within society but our point here is that capitalist incentives etc. are hegemonic and are expanding their reach into facets of daily life and social relations once seen as outside the economy.

14 The public policy literature discussed in Appendix 4.1 highlights the importance of the difference between outputs and the outcomes, or effects, of those outputs. Public policy is clearly more concerned to produce outcomes more than just outputs. Adopting the same framing, our use of the terms is that performances produce outputs but the network attributes value (it validates output) based on social outcomes. However, as will become apparent, it is necessary that ledgers record outputs, but these are always validated outputs (that is, they are recognized as having produced certain outcomes). When we describe the social contribution of performances, the focus will be on outcomes; when we describe the ledger processes, the focus will be on outputs, but the latter always presumes network-validated outcomes. This process is described in Chapter 4.

Reciprocal staking. All agents invest in other agents. They invest not from a store of 'money,' but by giving up stake in themselves. Hence staking is reciprocal. The network will involve an evolving web of connections of stake ownership, creating the conditions for a network commons.[15] Agents therefore have financial, strategic and emotional skin-in-the-game across the network. Individual agents want their performances – their offers to the network – to be evaluated by the network as to whether they are deemed to create value for the network, and this evaluation determines the rewards for staking ('dividends').

New modes of valuing. When agents reciprocally stake and make their specific staking decisions on who in the network is creating valuable social output, they are signaling what they believe creates a 'collectively defined value.'[16] This signaling will be formed into network-generated units of measurement (see Chapter 7), so that agents in the network are participating in both creating value and defining what constitutes a 'collectively defined value.'

These three features are interrelated in ways that will unfold in subsequent chapters. In effect, we have taken the collective values of the commons and designed a way to reconcile them with market relations.

Our goal is to build distributed economic relations that privilege collectively-expressed values and the creation and distribution of outputs (and their outcomes) that comply with, and are motivated by, those values. So the significance of starting with performances is that it gives focus to *shared flows of value creation*, and the incentives to risk in generating those flows, not on the issue of *individual decisions to buy and sell*.

---

15 The way in which mutual staking forms a commons is addressed in Chapter 6.

16 In the focus on alternative notions of value, staking could be seen as an act of partial or full philanthropy. In that framing, the staker may simply want the performance and its outputs to be realized because they are a 'good cause.' The network will indeed collect data on these philanthropic stakings, and there may appear correlations/causations that reveal a wider social benefit attributable to such performances. These performances may indeed find recognition in the network as value-creating, even when this is not the intention of the performing agents. But the network is not defined by philanthropy: it is defined by value creation and returns for value creation, where the distinctive feature is that the products of performances can create collectively defined value even when they create no profit.

This focus is the key to building a network with a collective momentum, rather than being a forum for trading per se.

1.4 A note on terminology

By this point, readers will have already come across some terms that are new, or familiar words being configured in new ways. In a project such as ours, it is always a dilemma whether to invent new terms or to try and wrest familiar terms from their narrow historic framings. We have done some of each, and carefully considered how to get that balance right. To assist readers in this interpretation, we provide a glossary to terminology developed in the Economic Space Agency.[17]

There are three terms, which have already appeared, that need some degree of clarification at this stage: staking, tokens and value. The clarification here is definitely preliminary, and we will reprise and elaborate these terms on a number of occasions as the analysis develops.

Staking. In cryptoeconomics, staking has recently become prevalent, but with multiple different points of emphasis. One use of the term arises in the context of 'proof-of-stake,'[18] where people stake their holdings of a token as collateral to become validators of ledger transfers of that token. A second form of staking is lending tokens that others may borrow (e.g. for use in derivative trades), generating a speculative yield to ownership. A third is collateralizing (staking) tokens for a loan in a stabletoken, which can then again be invested or staked (and the process rinsed and repeated, many times). These practices led to token markets becoming increasingly leveraged, and susceptible to the price crash that happened in 2022.[19]

A fourth use of the term staking involves locking tokens to a protocol's staking contract in return for certain 'rights.'[20] As a type, this form of staking is one application of our use of the term. In our analysis, staking involves taking on a financial exposure to the success/failure of another person or group's (agent's) creation of output. In aggregate, it gives a

---

17 The ECSA Glossary is available at https://glossary.ecsa.io/.
18 The need to cut energy usage in ordering transactions on a blockchain has seen the system of verification shift rapidly from proof-of-work to proof-of-stake.
19 Staking, in this sense, is often also incentivized by (often absurd) returns in the protocol native token, or in the protocol's native token in combination with some other protocol's token.
20 For example, vote-escrowed governance tokens, or some other 'rights,' largely depending on the amount and the length of staking time.

network a shared exposure to the future. It is a process of investing in new performance, and it generates returns based on the success of that process. Some in cryptoeconomics (e.g. Walden 2020) talk of the importance of intertemporal commitment in an 'ownership economy', and our view broadly aligns with this.

Tokens. By definition, tokens are an exclusive, transferable and quantifiable set of rights, but in many people's initial understanding, they are simply alternatives to the state's fiat currency, with bitcoin as the chief referenced challenger. In both cases, these are issued centrally by a third party. The state's issuance rests on the reputation of the state; bitcoin's on a widespread belief in the blockchain, its finite quantum and its cultural statement. Both are believed (and agreed) to be a store of value; one (for now) deemed 'safe'; the other volatile, but a store nonetheless.

The tokens we introduce are neither centrally issued nor do they store wealth in themselves: there is no 'money' in the conventional sense. Instead, in a distributed network (without a central 3rd party authority), tokens are issued by individuals/collectives (agents) to transfer an exclusive set of rights to an underlying value, be it a good, a service or an asset. Tokens are at the service of a ledger, and the balance on the ledger records the good service or asset being transferred in one direction and a token transferred in the other direction. The question, of course, is what you can do with a token issued by another person. Answering this will take us into details our analysis is not yet ready to reveal but, to give some answer, those tokens are associated with the settlement of credit.[21]

Value. This concept has two general meanings. One relates to values as an ethical frame (as in personal values). The other relates to value as a quantifiable statement of what something is worth. Those two may overlap significantly (a quantified ethics), but the second concept of value has a meaning as a unit of commensuration (or foundation for establishing equivalence), as in Marx's 'labor theory of value.' There, the term may be used in relation to the system of value calculation and analysis, or to the quantified worth of a particular thing (the value of/attributed to a cup of coffee, according to the adopted theory of value). We note the importance of the first, ethical meaning but do not discuss it, although we take it as the impulse to frame value theory in a particular way. In our analysis, we use the term value to mean both the abstract system of calculation, and the concrete valuation of particular outputs. However, it needs to be

---

[21] This issue is addressed in Chapter 7.

said that theories of value, of all varieties, perform best as indicative of social processes rather than formal calculative systems.

1.5 Capitalist and postcapitalist finance

Earlier in this chapter we gave focus to finance as the frontier of capitalist economic change and from where postcapitalism must develop. We then shifted to our own priority of building postcapitalist performances of value creation. So how do we frame the connection from capitalist frontiers of finance to a postcapitalist economy of value-creation? This connection forms the substance of the rest of this book, but our path into it starts by depicting the difference between capitalism and postcapitalism as a financial 'spread.'

The core questions that define the financial spread are:

- What counts as liquidity?
- What counts as collateral?
- What counts as 'surplus' and
- Who decides each of these?

The liquidity question. Who has the right to issue? In capitalism liquidity is about the state, the banking system it superintends and the money it endorses. When only those state-approved agents can issue, then a liquidity premium (a rate of return on money) can be charged for the risks involved in holding illiquid assets, because an exchange may not be found quickly.[22] The new economic space challenges this hegemony as the source of money issuance, proposing instead p2p reciprocal issuance amongst agents in a network. But what they issue is not 'money' as conventionally understood. Tokens in the network we propose are not private money, but claims on other agents: offers from one agent that are accepted by another and registered by the transfer of a token. Where all agents can issue in this sense, there need be no network shortage of liquidity and hence no liquidity premium.[23] The provision of liquidity can be fully collateralized by stake, and this collateral, rather than a liquidity

---

22 Stripped to its basics, the liquidity premium is a cost that addresses the deepest, darkest fear of capitalism: that the market (people to sell to or buy from) will simply disappear in sufficient numbers so that the flow will stop. This point, and the necessity of the dealer function, has been emphasized to us by Colin Drumm (2021), see also Treynor (1987).

23 For explanation see López, J. 'Market credit: Distributed liquidity protocol.' http://marketcredit.manifold.one

premium, covers lending risk.[24] Because collateral derives from the process of reciprocal staking it is the network overall that carries default risk. Stake becomes the complement of liquidity.

The collateral question. Who gets to determine what 'assets' are, and how they can be utilized for leverage? In capitalism, asset prices, and hence value as collateral, are linked to their capacity to generate future profit. Workers' primary asset – their capacity to work – is only collateral in the context of slavery and student debt. In the new economic space, agents' performances that create 'value' (as defined collectively by the network) forms the basis of collateral, for stake price is linked to value creation. In capitalism it is the capacity to create profit that defines stake as collateral; in postcapitalism, it is the capacity to create collectively defined value that defines stake as collateral. And because performances will be undertaken within non-extractive work relations, all participants have a stake and hence a claim to collateral.

The surplus question. What proportion of output is in excess of the costs of producing it, and who lays claim to the excess? The former is a measurement question; the latter the social access (class) question. Historically the determination of surplus was a process of extraction. In slavery and feudalism the surplus is that output in excess of the costs of sustaining slaves or a peasant class of producers. It is predominantly a surplus in the form of goods and services. In capitalism surplus is a financial concept because it is implied that all the components of output and hence the 'excess' can be commensurated, via units of value.[25] Surplus takes the financial form of rent, interest or profit.[26] Postcapitalism opens the question of how a surplus is to be defined (how costs and outputs are to be specified and measured: units of value and the unit of exchange) and claims of access to this surplus. In particular, where value is not defined by reference to profit, (some part of) surplus may be attributable to a commons.

---

24 This is the practice of shadow banking. Many people equate shadow banking with illegality. But investment banks like Goldman Sachs, insurance and reinsurance companies and money market funds – many of which are divisions of large 'standard' banks – engage in shadow banking, where the feature of being outside standard regulation is that lending is fully collateralized.

25 A unit of value will be explained in Chapter 6.3. Suffice it here to define it as a socially/historically specific system of measurement.

26 There can be an argument that the concept of 'profit' is not specific to capitalism; what is specific is the way profits are calculated. We have chosen to adopt the word 'surplus' in relation to the Economic Space Protocol to avoid ambiguity. See Appendix 5.2 for elaboration.

The 'who gets to decide?' question. 'Who has financial power?' is the financial version of 'class.' In capitalism, wealth and power are expressed critically in the capacity to decree the issuance of money and the valuation of assets.[27] In postcapitalism, all agents can issue assets to be used as collateral, other agents in the network have the capacity to accept these assets as collateral, and all collateral can serve to back liquidity. Implicit here is the idea that a postcapitalism, when framed through finance, can be depicted as an economy of abundance. This is not in the sense that too many commodities are produced, or that no-one will want for anything, but that when 'value' has diverse forms (not just profit-based) and is determined via distributed processes, we will all discover an abundance of economic activity, verified by a plethora of economic data analytics, which was hitherto performed without social recognition, and thereby no doubt under-performed.

We have mentioned the speed of change in cryptoeconomic history. Decentralized Finance (DeFi) has already introduced stablecoins as mechanisms for token exchange rate stability with respect to fiat currencies and pooling mechanisms for stabilizing token prices. More recently, it is introducing to cryptoeconomics the possibilities of distributed banking and insurance: that assets need not lie idle, but can be mobilized for borrowing and lending and with mechanisms of insurance offered on the side. The emergence of a rapidly-growing market for Non-Fungible Tokens (NFTs) is further accelerating this development, creating marketable assets whose sale creates collateral for further rounds of lending. Lending is then giving rise to the potential for leverage: borrowing in order to take positions in markets. That, in turn, is opening up issues like collateral requirements with margin calls and default risk. Predictably, we are already seeing the issuance of derivative financial products like credit default swaps (CDS) and collateralized debt obligations (CDOs) designed to on-sell default risk from those who wish to avoid it to those prepared to carry it for a fee.[28]

---

27 We note the blurring of the categories of money and assets. One form of blurring is between debt (money) and equity (assets) (e.g. convertible bonds). Another is found in central bank policies of Quantitative Easing, and the expanding range of assets central banks are taking onto their books in the name of 'monetary policy.' The blurring was noted by Myron Scholes (1997) in his Nobel Prize lecture.

28 Toporowski (2010: 12) puts it succinctly: 'in an era of finance, finance mostly finances finance.'

We can note in passing that these latter developments have the hallmark of the sorts of derivative products being traded in the lead-up to the 2007 global financial crisis. Whether they are pointing to crypto's 'Minsky moment'[29] 'is another matter, for the products themselves were never the source of crisis; it was their governance, expressed in pricing models and the conditions of access to leverage they were built upon. It is not surprising, therefore, that the emergence of 'crypto-derivatives' and a focus on DeFi governance are emerging concurrently. Whether they are emerging compatibly remains to be seen.

Nonetheless, we should note the enormous potential in the development of NFTs as derivatives on performances. The current focus in relation to NFTs creating a market for digital images should not obscure the potential to frame performances – value creating processes – as NFTs, and hence the ownership of NFTs as a financial exposure to the processes of future value creation. The relative simplicity of their issuance could open up a vastly new vision of how NFTs could be central tools of social innovation.

What sorts of derivative products might be exchanged in the new economic space? The answer is that there could be any and all of the above: agents can offer for exchange whatever they decide to. Governance of the network must be cognisant of the potential for 'Minsky moments.' In general, our interest is in derivatives that embed the social. We invoke, after Randy Martin, the 'social logic of the derivative.'[30] As 'the social' in the new economic space is conceived as a network, we will use the term 'network derivatives.' This means taking the logic of financial derivatives (futures, options and swaps)[31] and giving them network application as a collective

---

29 Named after economist Hyman Minsky, a 'Minsky moment' is a sudden collapse of asset values which becomes self-perpetuating. Collapses in asset values collapses the value of collateral leading to margin calls and the sudden loss of capacity to support loans.

30 Randy Martin was a friend and mentor to many of us in ECSA. He has inspired our vision and our analytical techniques. Randy died before the real emergence of crypto technology. His brilliance would have at once embraced the social and political potential of cryptomedia choreographies. See, for example, Martin (2013, 2014a, 2014b, 2015) and Lee and Martin (2016).

31 In finance, a derivative involves the purchase of an exposure to the 'value' of an underlying asset without (necessarily) purchasing ownership of the underlying asset itself. Derivatives therefore trade risk positions: the risk of the price of a barrel of oil going up or down, without trading the barrel of oil. Options, as critical forms of derivative, enable the coverage of risk in one direction, but not the other: they can insure against

value creating process. Here, the emphasis is on decomposed 'things' conventionally conceived as singular into their exposures (information, potentials and risks) so that they may be reconfigured as new creative directions. They enable the network to take positions on what counts as value, what counts as collateral and how liquidity creates social connection.

In particular, our financial approach to derivatives requires designing the optimal combination of price-determination conditions (what conventional economics calls decision-making under uncertainty) and flow-of-value conditions (what Marxism calls accumulation). When we get that balance right, we can target the ways to depict positions (decision-making) on social volatility (a flow). In effect, we are defining the potential of a spread in which agents risk. Expressed as stake choices and value creation, it sees agents making *individual* decisions to embrace a *social* conception of what is valuable.

1.6 The immediate proposal: living in the spread

Our proposal is framed in the spread between the network capacities of the current capitalist economic system and those of the Economic Space Protocol.

We have seen people active in art and design, the p2p movement and open source software engineers show close interest in our proposal, and we feel confident that the appeal of our vision will spread as its insights are understood. The proposition is not that we will simply 'transfer' to the new economy, but that we can spend part, and a growing part, of our economic lives in the new economic space.

Financially, we can frame capitalism and postcapitalism as a spread. Investing in the new economic space is trading the spread, taking a long position of an alternative to capitalist modes of valuing. But we also depict it as a short position: those who recognize pointers to capitalism's loss of legitimacy may want to place a bet against capitalism. Bitcoin may be a short position on capitalist money. Our proposal offers a short position on the capitalist economy and culture.

Our aspiration is that people will traverse the spread by being drawn towards participation in our postcapitalist vision and, in so doing, will in some degree reduce their current engagement with capitalism. Our hope is that more and more people will spend more and more of their time

---

prices going up, *or* they can insure against prices

engaging with and through the Economic Space Protocol. But in reality, we will be *living inside the spread.*

But we must conclude this introduction with a caution. All the above propositions assume the citizen capacities of liberal democracies and, within those democracies, there is the presumption that states will not regulate so as to subvert the development of proposals such as those of the new economic space. The threat of subversion-by-regulation points to a general political struggle for the right to think and organize differently, without denying the importance of the principle of the rule of law. We also understand that, in certain societies, distributed protocols, for all their internal stateless organization, are under the surveillance and control of centralized states intent on enforcing ideological compliance. In these places, there is no capacity to 'live in the spread.' These serious concerns point to a politics-beyond-choice; to forms of fascism. We emphasize our opposition to these regimes, and note that the struggle against them is a struggle for us all.

APPENDIX 1.1

DESIGN PRINCIPLES OF THE NEW ECONOMIC SPACE

The socioeconomic principles of the new economic space are:

- *Postcapitalist.* Economic protocols that can enable a progressive development beyond capitalism that use the devices of markets and finance to enable interoperability between contemporary capitalism and the new economic space.
- *Open.* An internet-native economic system with internet architecture; with no central data broker, host or owner.
- *Unified.* The systemic layer of unification becomes the economic grammar (the Economic Space Protocol) that enables transparent economic communication and empowers every agent equally. The social layer of unification to be designed through financial contracts.
- *Power-symmetric.* All agents in the system have the same default capacities (they can fully express through all the capacities of a shared economic language). This is the precondition for production to be organized through reciprocal economic relations and the pursuit of collectively-agreed outcomes, devoid of embedded or encoded extractive relations.
- *Socially valuable.* The capacity to express both tangible and intangible production processes by encoding them as 'performances,' and to benchmark all performances to an agreed measure of the social good.
- *Harnessing change.* Open-ended exposure to the potential of change. This entails embracing and harvesting volatility; not designing it away.
- *Equitable.* The risks and rewards of innovation must be distributed across the network in intentional and rightful ways.
- *Risk-sharing.* We aspire to 'risk together,' but in a measured way – in the sense of being both quantified and strategic. The long position may be risk taking, but the strategy itself needs to be low risk. This implies focussing on both the upside and downside of risk and the desire for individual choices within a 'together' strategy.

- *Economically interoperable.* The new economy will require a bootstrapping phase, centered on the conversion of capital market funds denominated in fiat into tokens to provide startup funds to new agents. Current economic forms can still be encoded in the new economic space, yet they can begin to actualize and experiment with the new tools.

APPENDIX 1.2

SOME KEY DISTINCTIONS BETWEEN THE ECONOMIC SPACE PROTOCOL AND OTHER PARADIGMATIC BLOCKCHAIN ARCHITECTURES.

Secrecy versus Privacy[32]

As an architecture, the Economic Space Protocol's approach to architecture is one where the protocol distributes records across a network of physical devices residing in different locations. There is no singular shared recording data structure, that is, the blockchain, but a network of nodes, each holding its records with remote references to those of others. Rather than relying on secrecy through cryptographically encoded records, it relies on privacy, where records start by being accessible only to their owner and located in the node where the owner created them. It is the owner who progressively shares them according to the logic of the network's protocol. So in the network there are private records, shared records, public records, and everything in-between. The protocol connects these records through remote references, creating a physically distributed data structure instead of relying on a partially encrypted globally replicated linked list as its recording medium.

Agents can determine which of their records they share at any point in time through offers (smart-contract offers) that outline how the information may be used by and through the network.

There is no need to pre-determine the bounds of the information that the network can collectively store, leaving it a programming choice. This architecture is necessary for the Economic Space Protocol, and the

---

32 See López, J. 'DJS: Distributed Javascript.' http://djs.manifold.one

economy it creates, as it keeps economic information private and economic instruments, distribution logics and performances, programmable. The architecture is thus very different to current blockchains and the token economies they enable.

Regulatory implications

The Economic Space Protocol does not rely on a discourse in which 'regulatory authorities' are to be evaded or avoided; instead, it empowers users by allowing them to determine key features of their agent's behavior: how it should be constrained or regulated through protocol; what information to share, and what information to keep private.

Are tokens securities?

Tokens in the Economic Space Protocol carry specific utility and are not passive investment vehicles. Although all agents in the network are issuers and holders, agents utilize tokens to enable their economic activity.[33] Tokens are functional and implement specific elements of the protocol.

Whether this will be subject to various states' regulation remains to be seen. However, we expect regulation only to be applicable in the on-ramp and off-ramp between the new economic space and the conventional economy.

---

33 For example, the liquidity token allows the user to exchange and clear commodity tokens. The stake token enables users to peer with others to create economic relationships through reciprocal mutual stakeholding.

CHAPTER 2

FROM CAPITALIST TO POSTCAPITALIST ECONOMY

2.1 Designing an economy

Is cryptoeconomy just a refinement and acceleration of a capitalist economy or can it create new economic space? It could be either or, indeed, both. The platforms that utilize blockchain and cryptographic technologies can be placed at the service of protocols that are essentially capitalist, or postcapitalist protocols that are conceived more cooperatively and commons-oriented – designed around shared aspirations, financial innovation and risking together. The technology permits both capitalist and postcapitalist versions to be designed centrally or in a distributed way. Importantly, framed this way, the postcapitalist agenda can be seen as no less practicable than a formally designed, distributed capitalism, and we can provide a clear depiction of *the difference* between the two. In both cases, there are cost and speed advantages of cryptoeconomic platforms because of the absence of need for central clearing houses, and we already see large corporations and states adopting the technology for fast, reliable, low cost and accurate record keeping. But there is a politics here, too. The emergence of central bank digital currencies is a stark statement.[34] It is not essential for states to digitally replicate their current money, but they realize they need a foothold in the space of crypto.

We are proposing the protocols of a postcapitalist economy in full awareness that this is a political as well as a technological project and, for us, that means that our analysis must be based in the lessons of history.

Our proposition, as it unfolds, points to the need to re-think some basic economic questions. We are not just opening the possibility of addressing new goals, and proposing more efficient ways of getting there.

---

34 The International Monetary Fund reports that, in 2022, 105 countries and currency unions are exploring central bank digital currencies (up from 35 in 2020; 19 of the richest 20 currencies are involved – see Fanti et al (2022)).

That would be to suggest that we know the end point. Rather, our objective is about network processes without specifying particular outcomes and hence without claims to their efficiency or harmony. We want to build the protocol on which *narratives of the future* can be built. We need to rethink what we mean by 'production' of value, where what constitutes 'value' is an open question, and where the motivations for engaging in, and staking, value creation are themselves as important as the outputs created. We need to reframe what markets are and what they could be as network relations without reference to profit and without a centralized operator. These dimensions will be revealed as the analysis unfolds.

2.2 An economics primer

While we are proposing to build an economy that is new in many respects, we cannot do so in a social, intellectual or historical vacuum. We must note what we can learn from capitalist modes of calculation, and we must engage an audience which may not have considered the possibility of building an economy on principles other than those identified with capitalism.

Accordingly, we turn to some basic principles of capitalist economics and start to focus on the ways in which they might (and might not) articulate with the potentials of a cryptoeconomy. In particular, our agenda is to pick apart certain standard economic categories in a detailed way, to ensure that we don't simply carry over concepts and approaches that will ultimately inhibit our project. But nor do we assume there is nothing to learn from the conventional knowledge. On the contrary, we need to blend the new with relevant lessons derived from the old.

Economics is a broad and contested discipline. It is also an old one, with Adam Smith's *Wealth of Nations* almost 250 years old, and Karl Marx's economics 180 years old. Back then it was debated as 'political economy,' with a narrower discipline of 'economics' – locking the social into a set of simplifying assumptions – dating only from the late 19th century. That narrowing involved the emergence of 'neo-classical' economics which remains hegemonic, more than 100 years on. It has, of course, significantly evolved over the past century, but the approach to 'the social' has varied little. It reduces the social to a set of behavioral abstractions (protocols), generally idealizations (*homo economicus* as their agent), which equate social goals with the operation of 'free' markets (businesses maximizing their profits; consumers maximizing their 'utility') and restrict the state's role to market facilitation. Theoretical innovations have generally been about adding complexity (e.g. game theory) and exploring 'distortions' (e.g. asymmetrical information; behavioral deviations from *homo economicus*). It presents as an *orthodoxy*, quite unlike the rest of the social sciences that are conceived in continuous theoretical and methodological debate. Moreover, it is not merely an orthodoxy but, as a socially decisive discourse, it is *performative*: this theory of markets and *homo economicus* are less an attempt to *describe society*, than an engineering effort to *remake society* in its own image, predicated on the assumptions of individualism, self-interest and the universal aspiration of profitability articulated through (predominantly) market relations. It has the template for the kinds of people and interactions it wants and, if permitted to run, it will find and train players to behave according to its model. In the era of cryptoeconomics we can describe this engineering effort as building protocols of social performance.[35]

But that orthodoxy is under new challenge, especially with the capacities of cryptocurrencies and cryptographically enabled distributed systems. We see the rise of a sub-discipline of 'cryptoeconomics' as a distinct field of analysis. However, we are concerned that the propositions of cryptoeconomics have so far engaged in a limited way in the social and political theory that lies behind their 'alternative' economics.[36]

Generally, challenges to the orthodoxy depict themselves as 'political economy', picking up on the 18th and 19th century recognition that economics and politics (the social) cannot be separated.

In modern usage, 'political economy' emerged in the 1950's as part of a radical rejection of capitalist class relations. Some branches reached back to Marx's propositions about the contradictions of capitalism and the emergence of a politicized working class to resist oppression, creating the way for a self-organizing society.

---

35 We already see, to quote Nick Land (2018, §2.653), if human beings are found to be irrational or incompetent or 'lack the plasticity to compete in these terms, or revolt against the roles and templates being automatically laid-out for them, then artificial agencies – 'DAOs' – will be fabricated to play the game instead.'

36 For example, Nick Szabo tweeted about economists and programmers: 'An economist or programmer who hasn't studied much computer science, including cryptography, but guesses about it, cannot design or build a long-term successful cryptocurrency. A computer scientist and programmer who hasn't studied much economics, but applies common sense, can.' @NickSzabo4, March 23 2018 https://twitter.com/nickszabo4/status/977035747713675264

Others developed a political economy that focussed on reforms of the state intended to make society fairer, more equal and more sustainable. Rather than a revolutionary politics, these reformers advocated a social democratic state, often looking to Scandinavian societies as their model.

Both schools of political economy lost potency in the 1980's and 90's. On the one hand, the fall of the Soviet Union and the 'marketisation' of China had reputational implications for Marxisms of all varieties, including those that despised the Soviet Union as much as they despised capitalism. On the other hand, the rise in the west of 'neo-liberalism' saw the state operating as the obstacle to 'progressive' reform, not as its agent. Simply advocating what a 'good' state *should* do lacked any real politics.

2.3 The Hayekian turn: knowledge, price and spontaneous order

But there was an emerging undercurrent of political economy, now coming from the 'right' of politics, that came to the fore in these contexts. It is most readily associated with the name Friedrich von Hayek – a rather marginal libertarian economist living in the shadow of Keynes and the (broadly) Marxists, but who came to public prominence in the 1970s as the theoretical guru of UK Prime Minister Margaret Thatcher: the person many attribute as the instigator of 'neoliberalism.'

We start with Hayek not because we see ourselves as being in the tradition of Hayek – quite the contrary – but because Hayek is so popular within the cryptoeconomic community. We will later have reason to draw on other economic traditions, especially Marx, Sraffa and Keynes. But in all cases the agenda is *not* to give a 'Hayekian,' 'Marxian' or 'Keynesian' take on cryptoeconomics: indeed we believe that the technologies of the internet, cryptography and a blockchain would have been challenging for all past thinkers and would have caused them to re-think some of their core analysis.[37] But what we can do is look at their methods (rather than their conclusions) and ask how these might be applied in the current era, to see what insights we can glean. Indeed, we conjecture that this framing will lead to conclusions often quite different from those that appear in the emerging cryptoeconomic literature.

Hayek was vehemently anti-socialist, but he had major conflicts with the neoclassical economists too. He embraced individual self interest as

---

37 Not least because these technologies exist in abundance, with marginal costs effectively zero.

the premise of social order but thought the neo-classicals adopted two positions he opposed.

First, he opposed their conception of 'equilibrium' as an optimal state. His preferred notion was 'spontaneous order.' That term might seem a close approximation of equilibrium, but the difference is critical. For Hayek, the quality of markets he affirmed was that they process complex information into simple information (prices). That is an intrinsic virtue, distinct from any claims that markets would somehow gravitate to balance or optimisation. It is the process that Hayek valued; not the outcome. Information processing is clearly critical to programming an economy; it is an issue to which we will return.

Second, Hayek opposed the conventional endorsement of the state in economic management. The state, he contended, is innately authoritarian, imposing its will on society: sometimes well-intentioned but flawed; other times clearly enhancing the power of the state itself.[38] The market, claimed Hayek, is the natural site of freedom of expression and a means to generate spontaneous social order.

Of course the popular critique is that markets, if left to themselves, create massive inequality, environmental destruction, etc.. Not so, said Hayek. It is the inadequate specification of property rights and the rules of markets (that we reveal as a distributed protocol) that are the problem, and when states tinker with outcomes (levies and bounties) they generally mess up. Most critically, they mess up the provision of a state-sanctioned money system (fiat money).

Not surprisingly, Hayek has had great appeal in cryptoeconomics. On the surface, they are a near perfect fit. A cryptoeconomic order conceived in a rejection of the state as economic manager, including as provider of the sole monetary system, and instead focussing on data analytics and optimizing individuals in contractual transactions, seems to resonate deeply with Hayek. So too does the idea, expressed in his *The Fatal Conceit* (1988), of the need to break up conventional, secure but distorting practices.

We can readily source essays on cryptoeconomics that celebrate the self-directed individual and claim foundations in Hayek.[39] It should be

---

38 Milton Friedman later called it the tyranny of the majority: that an elected government could claim legitimacy in trampling on people's natural rights. For some, quadratic voting offers an alternative.

39 Albeit that they tend to ignore the later Hayek's more nuanced view of markets, and the recognition that the state always plays critical roles of market facilitation.

noted that, knowingly or not, the idealization of individualism, profit and the market as foundational social relations come as integral to the Hayek package and those foundations are being transmitted, perhaps not always intentionally, into cryptoeconomic culture. This adoption leaves unquestioned the issues of what we count and how we measure: both of which embody the potentially transformative politics of cryptoeconomics.

In creating new economic space, we are opening the opportunity for a different economic calculus. Our proposition is that knowledge, prices and their relation to markets need to be re-thought. What Hayek and conventional economics, and their digital disciples, take as foundational in relation to markets, we think are protocols. As protocols, they are designable in different ways. But Hayek and his followers seem to think not. They analyze 'the market' as a platform: culturally foundational and economically 'natural.' For them, the market is depicted as a neutral technology into which individuals bring their strategic interests and which, if allowed to operate as it 'should,' will create 'equilibrium' (neoclassical economics) and 'spontaneous order' (Hayek). The social 'good'/'harm,' the commons, the environment, that sit outside these individual interests can only be framed as 'externalities,' and hence second order considerations.[40]

What stands as contestable, and where we will focus our analysis, is the question of what we mean by 'markets,' 'price mechanisms' and their relations with 'society.' Markets are socially constructed, not 'natural,' and they embed particular social protocols. Markets transmit a range of information; not just price. Moreover 'price' itself transmits information, but it is always encoded in a particular way of measuring. So markets, as spaces of exchange, need not relate to profit, but can be designed to generate the sorts of information a network needs. As they currently are utilized, they are fundamentally directed to serving the pursuit of profit-making. In summary, market processes are not innately capitalist and their logic is not innately extractive (expressing social dominance).

If we can isolate the process of market interactions from a social context of wealth, power and inequality, and redesign them at the center of a

---

40 There are current critiques of capitalism that feature the proposition that capitalist markets ignore 'externalities' (costs and revenues that are not allocated within existing property relations). The classic case is pollution, which imposes social costs that are not borne by the polluter. We concur that this failure is significant, but contend that if we focus on this 'flaw,' then we are implicitly conceding that, in the absence of externalities, capitalist markets warrant our affirmation. Our critique is that they privilege profitability and individualism over other values and collective benefit, whether or not there are externalities.

distributed postcapitalist economy, they can be seen as means of voting for economic outcomes, articulating individual views about what constitutes value. Issues of social benefit and harm, the environment, etc. in capitalism must be either contrived into profit calculus or treated as 'externalities,' and essentially outside of market calculus. We want to bring them inside market calculus by adapting market processes to value the things that we know to be socially important, but which are left out of capitalist markets. We shouldn't conflate markets-under-capitalism with markets-as-information-transmission processes.

In the new economic space, markets are explicitly defined by distributed network protocols. They are spaces of exchange and valuation: they structure the space of possibilities for interactions and for the economic properties of the objects populating such spaces. A market is a network and is defined by offer, matching, netting and clearing protocols that its agents must adopt in order to interoperate as a coherent whole.

2.4 Hayek's dead end

To get to the logic of the new economic space we don't simply go via a simple refutation of Hayek, for his emphasis on markets as mechanisms of information collection and transfer is important. It is worth teasing out Hayek's view so as to subsequently clarify what is distinctive about the new economic space.

In the mid 20th century, Hayek and his Austrian School colleagues opened a debate with advocates of (broadly) Soviet-style planning. It became known as the Socialist Calculation Debate. Here is not the place to review that debate, although it warrants noting that there is a recent literature riffing off it to address the emergent computational capacities for efficient large-scale central planning.[41]

Hayek's proposition, which is hard to refute in historical context, is that Soviet central planning was always authoritarian and operating with inaccurate and outdated data when making resource allocation decisions. It was, at the time, an easy critique given the level of Soviet information technology and a war-ravaged economy, although the debate drew some creative interventions about how central planning might be integrated

---

41   See Bernes (2020), for an impressive recent contribution. Some have argued that global corporations are applying all the techniques that would be required for state-run central planning. See, for example, Phillips and Rozworski (2019).

with market processes in a combination known as 'market socialism.'[42] Some of these interventions, applying neo-classical economic criteria of efficiency, were more challenging for Hayek to refute, but his argument always came back to the point that markets provide superior information and enable the pursuit of individual freedom (read self-interest).

In the context of the Socialist Calculation Debate, Hayek made statements about markets and information that have clearly resonated in cryptoeconomics. It is worth quoting Hayek at some length:

> It is in this connection that what I have called the 'economic calculus' proper helps us, at least by analogy, to see how this problem can be solved, and in fact is being solved, by the price system. Even the single controlling mind [the central planner], in possession of all the data for some small, self-contained economic system, would not—every time some small adjustment in the allocation of resources had to be made—go explicitly through all the relations between ends and means which might possibly be affected. It is indeed the great contribution of the pure logic of choice that it has demonstrated conclusively that even such a single mind could solve this kind of problem only by constructing and constantly using rates of equivalence (or 'values,' or 'marginal rates of substitution'), i.e., by attaching to each kind of scarce resource a numerical index which cannot be derived from any property possessed by that particular thing, but which reflects, or in which is condensed, its significance in view of the whole means-end structure. In any small change he will have to consider only these quantitative indices (or 'values') in which all the relevant information is concentrated; and, by adjusting the quantities

---

42 Market Socialism sought to integrate private enterprise or capitalist modes of calculation within socialist planning, generally by the operation of markets at the 'local' level, with market information guiding central planners in the 'big' allocation decisions. This intervention in the Socialist Calculation Debate is associated especially with Ota Šik, economist and deputy Prime Minister of Czechoslovakia, who was central to the liberalization of the Czech economy and the 'Prague Spring' that triggered the Soviet invasion in 1968. Capitalist modes of calculus, via the use of changes in stocks rather than prices to determine output decisions, is associated with post-war Polish economist Oskar Lange.

Our concern is not balance between planning and markets, for we believe it to be a false juxtaposition, but with the protocols under which markets are conceived. But it should be noted that this literature precipitated Hayek's break with neo-classicals: both their conception of 'competition' and their belief in 'equilibrium.'

one by one, he can appropriately rearrange his dispositions without having to solve the whole puzzle *ab initio* or without needing at any stage to survey it at once in all its ramifications.

Fundamentally, in a system in which the knowledge of the relevant facts is dispersed among many people, prices can act to coördinate the separate actions of different people in the same way as subjective values help the individual to coördinate the parts of his plan. (Hayek 1945: 225-26)

So Hayek has identified a critical issue: that markets, as a protocol, construct indices of measurement, in this case a rate of exchange, so that any small component of the economy can be commensurated against the whole, for this is the condition of tracing how a change in that small thing impacts the whole. This is an issue we return to consistently: the construction of distinctly postcapitalist communication networks and ways of measurement.

Hayek's notion of 'free' markets and prices transmitting information may be one technical 'solution' (if we leave to one side the conceptually trivial and therefore socially dangerous idea of 'free' markets[43]), but it is only one, and a decidedly capitalist, 'solution.' For Hayek, price is the reduction of complexly-layered knowledge to a single index. With everyone speaking the language of price and the pursuit of profit as a singular objective for decision-making, market interactions are said to generate spontaneous order, but what they actually do is to structure the space of the possible. Hayek's mid 20th century advocacy of 'the market' and trust in 'prices' may stand strong as an alternative to Soviet central planning, but 75 years on the argument must be different.

It is important to understand that alternative economic indexes can be based in different knowledge, producing a different logic: a different space of what is possible. We want indexed movements to measure economic performance(s) and surpluses and to trigger trading strategies for agents that lead to wider economic decisions about what is produced and how. We want to avoid automatic reliance on indices that embed profit maximizing strategies or situate in monetary processes driven by interest extraction. We depict our preferred measures as the performance indices of the new economic space. Performance indices are explored in Chapter 4.

---

43 Hayek's explicit reference to a means-end structure signals that the ends are beyond evaluation.

We should note the way in which Hayek depicts price as a simplified index that obviates the need for agents to hold full knowledge. Via cultural enmeshment, agents come to believe that price can be trusted to incorporate knowledge.

> The most significant fact about this system is the economy of knowledge with which it operates, or how little the individual participants need to know in order to be able to take the right action. In abbreviated form, by a kind of symbol, only the most essential information is passed on, and passed on only to those concerned. It is more than a metaphor to describe the price system as a kind of machinery for registering change, or a system of telecommunications which enables individual producers to watch merely the movement of a few pointers, as an engineer might watch the hands of a few dials, in order to adjust their activities to changes of which they never know more than is reflected in the price movement. (Hayek, 1945: 526-27)

It would be a misrepresentation of Hayek to read from this quote that prices are the *only* data on which agents make decisions: after all, no-one buys anything simply because of its price. Price may initiate exchange as the trigger information, but it is not sufficient information to explain exchange.[44] Individuals are also 'readers' of themselves and of the 'market conditions' and they trade on the basis of their subjective preferences, informed by whatever information they choose to utilize. The brilliance of markets, he thought, is the reduction of a complexity of data to a single index of exchange.[45] Through price signals, markets transmit 'tacit' or 'dispersed' knowledge. But, for all the information individuals may potentially generate – including their affects and velleities[46] – it is only the transaction-at-a-price that triggers a data entry.

In Hayek's framing, price may be the condensation of a complex set of knowledges, but knowledge is not intended to be reverse engineered

---

44 Morozov (2019) contends it is just a neoclassical interpretation of Hayek that argues *all* information reduces to price.

45 For example, when I pay $5 for a cup of coffee I am not actually going through a complex calculation of the costs of all the technologies, raw materials, transport, labor, taxes, consumer preferences etc. that lie behind a cup of coffee. I just reduce all that to the acceptance of the price, pass over the debit card, and receive the coffee.

46 This is the perfect word in this context, but it is not in common usage, so we offer a definition. A velleity is a wish or inclination not strong enough to lead to action.

from price.[47] All other data about an output and the interactions around its creation and exchange are thereby lost when price is elevated as the form in which knowledge is transmitted. Yet we now know that, in the current world, social media and on-line marketing are assembling all sorts of data about individuals, their velleities, 'attributes' and networks. In these 'attention markets' price is just one amongst many data points valued by corporations. A postcapitalist economy not driven by extractive relations or surveillance, will nonetheless need data-rich architecture. This issue is taken up in Appendix 2.1

Price is not the condensation of knowledge. Price is, after all, no more than one index: it measures *relative* exchange values (between commodities; over time). But in the hands of Hayek (and the neo-classicals), with their version of 'the market' naturalized as a platform, price can be treated socially as an *absolute* social measure. Indeed this is the analytical objective: to create the impression that price formation is the social expression of the natural order of markets. Prices slide from being technically relative values framed in a particular social and economic context to being presented as socially absolute values.

Here is where many crypto analysts who profess dissent from capitalist values get unwittingly trapped: by celebrating the creation of a monetary system freed from the state, but embracing the reliance on markets and self interest they embed the values they are seeking to escape. How we frame markets, prices and units of account are the central economic questions of a distributed postcapitalist economy.

2.5 Prices freed from profit

Our starting point is that information must 'from the start' be an expression of social values, in the same way that Hayek's information 'from the start' expresses capitalist values. Our postcapitalist network will require data on flows of intentions, affect and emotional commitments – expressions of the sorts of values that will frame the direction of this economy – for these data will inform the debates and choices about making that future.

Prices in a capitalist economy are determined, generally, by the interaction of supply and demand. Demand may be all about individual 'tastes': their values, aesthetics, needs, etc.: a domain generally inaccessible to economics, except as data. Supply in a capitalist economy is more

---

47 Financial market models that attempt this reverse engineering are at best crude, and were not envisioned by Hayek.

telling. It is dictated, other than in exceptional cases, by the condition of profitability. Whether adopting a competitive market explanation or a post-Keynesian mark-up (cost plus a rate of profit) explanation of prices, profitability is at the center. Producers will not supply to a market unless it is profitable to do so.[48] The value of capital assets are defined by their profit-generating potential, and so on.

Further, prices-linked-to-profit are based in the way profit is calculated, and that points to the structure of accounting. There exists an extensive literature in the history of accounting, tying the system of double entry book-keeping to the rise of capitalism.[49] Double entry book-keeping, as it developed, became central to the way wealth is specified as 'capital'; how profit (the extraction of a surplus from production by the owners of capital) became legitimized by the mode of its inclusion into the structure of corporate accounts, and how the concept of 'profit' evolved as capitalism itself has evolved.[50]

A postcapitalist economy cannot adopt capitalist modes of accounting. Yet, in parallel with our contentions about prices and markets, it is important to differentiate the particular capitalist application of double entry ledgers – the units in which measurement is recorded – from the logic of ledgers formulated with a system of entries and counter-entries. The use of tokens and a ledger-based accounting system are central to the Economic Space Protocol and in later chapters we will explore the way in which an economic space, with double entry book-keeping measured with a different units of value, opens the possibility for a different determination of 'prices' and designation of a surplus, and how these link to designing postcapitalist value.

Indeed, as will be explained in Chapter 4, combinations of information, and propositions of their economic significance (what we call 'performances'), come to the fore as the critical, frontier products of the new economy. Giving meaning (even competing meanings) to information is

---

48 We note the short term supply condition of covering fixed costs, so ours is a longer-term and more general proposition.
49 The work of R.A Bryer is particularly important in this analysis. See https://www.researchgate.net/scientific-contributions/RA-Bryer-2003195221. For a summary of and insight on the literature accounting and capitalism, see Chiapello (2007) and Chapter 6.3.
50 Indeed, it was not until the middle of the 19th century and the rise of joint stock companies (ownership diversified through a stock exchange), that the rules of these accounts became generalized. In essence, owners and prospective owners needed reputable information on which to base their decisions to buy and sell.

the critical economic agenda for the future. This is about using information to create narratives of the future, as a way of opening up new possibilities, rather than codifying data into price for individual market choices. Why then is 'price,' as it is currently measured, the privileged index of valuation? Why do we not use (for example) sociality (social impact) as the privileged index of valuation? Or environmental impact? The answer is that these issues are not currently being tracked in the records (the ledgers) on which the current economy operates.

We are interested in focusing on the richness of information *flows* and not just with the specific indices ('prices') that get generated as part of the flows. And we want 'price' (or the quantum attributed to an output which has been validated by the network through market expression) to itself express 'social values'; not profit per se.

2.6 Turning Hayek on his head

The challenge we've mounted is to make clear that the process of price formation 'price,' as it is conventionally understood, can be re-framed as just one set of protocols but not, as Hayek would have us believe, the *only* one. In the context of distributed ownership and distributed issuance of 'money,' the social processes of the economy will be profoundly challenged.

Three challenges are pivotal, and they drive the analytical agenda of our analysis:

Network value. How does a network place a value on outputs not produced for sale in a market, for example an art display, creating green spaces, new open source technology and human care?[51] Outputs-with-no-price cannot be interpreted in a Hayekian framing. Our preferred approach comes not via value in exchange, but via how agents in the network place a value on the performances which produce the outputs. We are interested in the *performance* of care; the *vision* of green space, the *potential* of open technology, and these cannot be framed in standard market analysis devoid of time, affect and contingency.

The role of the Economic Space Protocol is to build ways to express the value of outputs, without reliance on a direct price (see Chapter 3.5.). Moreover, those who create outputs-with-no-price should participate in rewards based on social assessment of their contribution. The reward

---

51 Of course these outputs *can* be designed for commercial sale, but that will capture only a fraction of their social contribution/collective value.

is to be understood simply as a share of a surplus created in production (see Chapter 5 and Appendix 5.2).[52]

Time. Hayek works with a limited conception of time as purely linear, clock time. In credit, interest accrues over time, but time itself is analytically passive. Investment is explained as a return to entrepreneurship and foresight. Capital is a riddle: 'Why,' asks Hayek (1941: 60), 'should the more time-consuming methods of production yield a greater return,' and he answers it by reference to the requirements of technical change in production. In each case, there is simply clock time, and its importance is only to compare rates of return.

A network requires a different conception of time, for time is the condition of contingencies and what matters is the sequence of events (what financial markets call 'tick time').[53]

In an exchange, the ledger-based processes of offers, matches, netting and clearing may all happen virtually instantaneously, as if timeless, but may take time to execute. Our analytical focus is the *duration*,[54] or on the set of state changes required for the exchange. It logically forms an interval, and within the duration of this interval, while certain mechanical processes may be risk-free, contingencies are critical.[55] In 'performances,' as we are framing them, this interval is occupied by the momentum for innovation, affect and social change. In standard analysis, these would be cast as 'subjective' and unmeasurable, though when they manifest in 'price' they suddenly become objective and measured. Tick time is defined by the rhythm of those momentums and dynamics: the focus is on

---

52 At this point in the analysis, a surplus can be taken to mean any excess over what is required to reproduce the current conditions of the network. It is usually thought in financial terms (profit rent, interest) or commodity outputs in excess of commodity inputs (e.g. Sraffa, 1960). We will later invoke broader, more social perspectives on 'surplus.'

53 See, for example Goldman Sachs analyst (later Professor of Financial Engineering at Columbia University) Emanuel Derman (2002) says of short-term investors: 'They may perceive and experience the risk and return of a stock in *intrinsic time*, a dimensionless time scale that counts the number of trading opportunities that occur, but pays no attention to the calendar time that passes between them.'

54 Reference here is to Henri Bergson's (1889) framing of duration, further developed by Deleuze (1988). The critical point is that the time of change and event cannot be reduced to its preconditions, thus going beyond a linear (and spatial) conception of time.

55 This process depicts the network as if it were, in key respects, an automated market maker: an agency which executes orders on behalf of agents in the network.

the repetition of occurrences and patterns.⁵⁶ It gives quantifiable access to the way in which people respond to a duration. More abstractly, and as we will explore in relation to units of account, tick time opens up the question of what is measured (what is deemed by the network as important to measure), how to measure it and the meanings of duration.

When we add time and contingency we open the conditions of a derivative framing not addressed by Hayek. In the era of blockchain and big data, and in the language of Gilles Deleuze we can 'dividuate' knowledge: break it down into its underlying, determining elements (that Hayek thought were too complex to code), but without necessarily aspiring to see those elements combined so as to ontologically privilege the totalized category of a singular 'knowledge,' linked to 'price.' Knowledge is a synthetic asset; an assembly of processed information. Its purpose does not have to be the formation of 'market price.'⁵⁷

Liquidity. In Hayekian analysis (and in conventional economic analysis) all markets are assumed to be liquid.⁵⁸ The presumption of liquidity is required in order to assume that there is a single price for any good or service: there will be no need to discount from normal prices to secure a trade. This assumption forms the foundation of financial pricing models and conceptions of efficiency, be it the efficient markets hypothesis, the capital asset pricing model or the Black Scholes Merton options pricing model. Marx's analysis also assumes liquidity: that buyers and sellers are in sufficient numbers to enable outputs to sell 'at their value.' The absence of liquidity is a definition of 'crisis.'

Where there are two prices – a bid-ask spread – it is unclear what is meant, in Hayekian discourse, by 'price,' and hence in the depth of knowledge that is said to condense into price.⁵⁹ A spread framed simply as two

---

56 In Marx's depiction of capitalism, this dynamic is expressed as the pursuit by capital of relative surplus value (growing profit from changing the conditions of production: a creative but nonetheless extractive logic). But if we take innovation out of the discourse of profit-seeking capitalism, it is the momentum to pursue many, diverse developments, consistent with the values expressed by the network, that will enable the expanded reproduction of the system.

57 It follows that we can think of Hayek's price as itself a derivative on those underlying forms of information of which price is said to be the condensate. In Hayek's analysis, 'price' is really the strike price on the option on a synthetic asset called 'knowledge.'

58 For Hayek, and Keynesian economics, the story of liquidity ties to agents' desires to hold liquid or illiquid assets and the capacity of the rate of interest to impact that choice.

59 In Marx, too, the existence of a bid-ask spread creates challenges in the depiction of price in relation to value. We thank Colin Drumm for this point.

prices points to inefficiency or distortion, not innovation (or an impossibility of telling the difference) and the momentum that gets focus is not the dynamic of innovation, but the dynamic of arbitrage and the process by which the spread closes. The point is that price risks are embedded in price but cannot be separated from price: a price alone cannot disclose the probability of the price changing, though a price spread can. Prices cannot be disentangled from derivatives of prices.

There is more here than this technical point, and our proposal needs to identify two critical factors.

First, in a network of mutual credit issuance (which is yet to be elaborated), liquidity is an index of sociality: the preparedness of agents to issue credit and make markets is an expression of social engagement and trust in network protocols. The basis of trust is not that the state monetary authorities or banks will 'do the right thing' in their policy discretion, but that there is knowledge that a) all credit is fully collateralized (Chapter 8); b) default risk will be spread across the network (because ownership is dispersed, see Chapter5) and c) all agents understand the liquidity requirements of others by understanding their own liquidity requirements (Chapter 8). A breakdown of liquidity, such as happened in the 2007-2008 financial crisis and the 2019-2022 pandemic crisis, is itself a breakdown of sociality because the centralized financial system highlighted the difference between individual interest (wanting to receive liquidity, but not give it) and collective interest. In a distributed economic system, all economic agents must take responsibility for the provision of liquidity, and performance indices must produce measures to verify the need for and conditions of liquidity. This is why the mutual issuance of credit is critical to the Economic Space Protocol, for it makes provision of liquidity and the distributed, not hierarchical, sociality of the network integrally related.

Second, markets will see bid-ask spreads that cannot be presumed to close in the time interval implicit in an automated market making function of the network. In an equilibrium framing, this is a market failure, where prices aren't adjusting to clear the market. But where the focus is on innovation, spreads are always opening up, the propensity is not towards balance, but dynamic change and the creation of a surplus by the network-as-a-whole. In the conventional analysis of a bid-ask spread, a profit is presumed to accrue by trading on the spread. In a postcapitalist network, the question to be addressed is: who lays claim to the surplus, and how can it be realized as a *social* surplus rather than a private one? This issue is addressed directly in Chapter 5.3 and Appendix 5.3.

2.7 Implications

We have gone through an engagement with Hayek (but also, indirectly, Marx, Keynes and others) to give focus to the proposition that markets and the prices they generate do not have to connect to profits, and profits are not the sole, nor indeed primary, measure of economic achievement. Our goal has been to contest these assumed links not just as an ethical stand in the name of social goals of equality and respect for the biosphere and humanity, but as an analytical proposition. We can 'unpick' the apparent logic that links individual interest to markets and markets to profits and 'design' market relations quite differently. They need not focus on prices, or profits or individuals, but they can generate information systems that can utilize indices other than price; a range of goals and of inter- and intra-agent relations. But they will still be markets markets – markets as communication networks. The objective of protocol design is to give an orderly opportunity to re-imagine the ways in which economic goals are set and measured. We are seeking to develop the protocols for utilizing network-generated data to keep social goals – multiple goals – at the forefront of calculative processes.

APPENDIX 2.1

DO 'BIG DATA' CHANGE THE STORY?

There is now a growing literature proclaiming that the emergence of big data is dramatically transforming, even abolishing capitalism (e.g. Zuboff, 2019). Often Hayek's work forms a point of departure. Viktor Mayer-Schönberger and Thomas Ramge, the authors of *Reinventing Capitalism in the Age of Big Data*,[60] for example, tell us that we no longer need to see all knowledge reduced to 'prices.' Directly-accessed data will supplement and in some ways supplant prices as the critical source of information. This, they say, challenges the role of money in a capitalist society.

We half agree. The standing of a unitary measure of price as the driver of exchange can and should be under challenge. Other metrics will themselves be indexified and those indices tokenized. Diverse tokens will express a 'market' for innovation in social valuation: a market potentially far more important than competition over prices.[61] But we do not agree that this is a challenge to the role of money, nor to capitalism itself.

---

60 We nominate this book amongst a range of recent contributions about the implications of big data for understanding the future of capitalism because of its claims to significance. The original German version is titled *Das Data*; a play on Marx's *Das Kapital*.

61 A parallel proposition in relation to capitalism is that competition for technical change (motivated by cost cutting, new product design, etc.) is of greater long-term significance than competition over prices in a market. Indeed, history shows that the great monopolies/oligopolies of history are defeated by being technologically superseded, not by competition from lower cost providers. We do not believe that data will somehow sit alongside price as an additional input to decision making, for within conventional calculus data will predictably be incorporated into pricing, and product design (and marketing) will become more differentiated in response to the patterned diversity revealed in data. We concur that the role of capitalist money will indeed be challenged. Yet the challenge will not be by recourse to an amorphous mass of statistics. It will occur via the invention of new, different indices: new modes of 'money' (tokens) expressing different social knowledges.

In popular debate, big data are framed as individual surveillance by corporations and states, and hence a privacy and civil liberties issue.[62] This, too, resonates with a Hayekian focus on the rights of individuals. Yet big data are also what national and international statistical agencies collect to enable a monitoring of dispersed processes in order to build an aggregate depiction of the economy, and to feed into economic policy formation. Clearly, the categories in which those data are assembled themselves embed a particular social and economic approach to society.[63] So there is an immediate contradiction that big data, cast as a digital record of 'the social,' will be used against society. For Hayek this combination of issues saw Soviet-style central planning as *The Road to Serfdom* (1944): that central control of data and planning was innately authoritarian and contrary to the rights and freedoms of individuals. We know that this understanding is not specific to mid 20th century so-called socialist planning: in the digital era there is a clear record of social media companies – including the largest global companies in the world – mining personal data and manipulating both individuals and political processes.

Conversely, Posner and Weyl (2018), in what they take to be the spirit of Hayek, advocate that individuals should own and trade their own data. From our perspective, people's ownership of their own data is fundamental, but the Posner and Weyl proposal is at most a second best alternative. Individuals may receive a fee for their data, but will then lose control over how those data are used once sold. It does not address the loss of control; it simply prices it.

Our preferred position, embedded in the protocol design of the new economic space, is that individual data are considered the property of individuals, but it is also recognized that pooled data are critical to identifying the health and dynamism of the network.

Instead of an individual data market, the new economic space proposes a data commons: individual agents can choose whether, and to what degree, to share their data with the commons, and in return acquire access (according to the degree of sharing) to the aggregate data of the commons.

---

62 See Chapter 4.4 for some consideration of internally-generated data, although this analysis is not intended as an engagement with social debates about big data.

63 Keynes wrote his *General Theory* (1936), which transformed economic policy in the mid 20th century, without use of data. His view was that the economic data which were collected at the time were assembled in taxonomies incompatible with his new theory. Empirical Keynesianism awaited the development of national accounts compiled in 'Keynesian' categories.

The protocols of the commons are considered in Chapter 6. In the current context, we note simply that mutual staking of a commons enables a distributed but shared position on economic design,[64] securing both individual rights of engagement and the benefits of co-operative endeavor.

---

64 Morozov (2019) has drawn attention to the seemingly-neglected work of Daniel Saros (2014). Saros develops important insights on the use of big data in decentralized planning. While written without reference to crypto and blockchain, it is clearly blockchain-relevant.

CHAPTER 3

MARKETS AS COMMUNICATION NETWORKS

3.1 Introduction

To build the conditions for a distributed postcapitalist economy it is clear that markets are integral: they are an essential source of information in a scalable, non-centralized system. But should an analysis of postcapitalism start with markets?[65] In Chapter 1 we contended that the Economic Space Protocol is centered on postcapitalist performances and the creation of collectively-defined meanings of value. Yet we are starting our exposition of this Protocol not with performances of new value creation but with processes of market exchange. This is not a matter of choice: it is the engineering foundation on which communication protocols must be built.

We share this entry point with Marx, in Volume 1 of *Capital* (1867), who starts by establishing the principles of equivalence in exchange, denominated in units of labor time – what he calls 'simple exchange' – before he turns to the production of new value. Like Marx, we later return to exchange in a central role; now within the dynamics of an economy of investing and credit issuance (Chapter 9). Some, including supporters of Marxism, would say that this starting point is fraught with problems,[66] for building the dynamism and uncertainty of performances on top of a

---

[65] Those who oppose market relations (and generally also the adoption of token exchange) generally also advocate localism, where it is direct personal relationships, not in a record-keeping system that form the basis of trust. The inevitable neglect of the production process that cannot exist without scale is clear, so this perspective is not engaged in our analysis. Furthermore, local relations are never without their own power relations.

[66] In Marxism, one way of depicting the so-called 'transformation problem' is the challenge of reconciling value defined in simple exchange with value defined in dynamic accumulation of capital.

protocol of simple exchange is challenging. Performances and exchanges have different drivers: they are not an automatic fit. But it is where we start, and we must approach it knowingly, including appreciating the challenges it created for Marx.[67]

In particular, it is important to recognize that the analysis in this chapter assumes a liquid market: that there are no impediments to transactions due to a lack of capacity to 'buy' (match an offer). This is a simplifying assumption to 'get the analysis rolling.' In Chapter 8 we return to issues of liquidity, in the context of bringing network credit into the analysis.

A challenge of starting with simple market exchange is that everyone thinks they know how exchange works, so our propositions will be read as just an idiosyncratic restatement of a familiar process. But this chapter is much more than a semantic re-framing of conventional depictions of markets: the explanation below opens up one face of the distinctive dynamics of the Economic Space Protocol. Just as exchange is different in gift societies from capitalist societies, so it is different in the new economic space. In this chapter, we address how market interactions have to be designed in order to be non-capitalist, scalable, with unique units of account and not centrally managed.

Here is a brief summary, with each word needing respecification in italics. Those who participate in *markets* are *agents* who interact in a *network* and, through their interactions, create *economic space*. In these markets, *prices* are disconnected from the presumption of pursuit of profit and instead express units of collectively-defined *network value* (see Chapter 13.2). Transactions are confirmed by the transfer of *tokens* on a network *ledger*, rather than exchanges of 'money.'

One particular condition is elevated by this reframing. It is critical to dissociate collectively defined value from sales and hence expenditure/revenue from sales. The new economic space must be able to attribute value to outputs produced for the commons, and those who produce collectively defined value for the commons must be able to receive a yield on their performance (as the condition of their reproduction). This means a network attribution of value for outputs that do not 'go to market.'

---

67 Critics of Marx would say that the need to reconcile every commodity's value denominated in labor time with a market price is the technical flaw in Marx's analysis: the so-called 'transformation problem.'

3.2 Agents and markets

Most introductions to economics depict 'individuals' interacting as buyers and sellers in predominantly monetized markets. The Economic Space Protocol depicts 'agents' in tokenized markets. What's the difference?

Agents

An economic agent is a networking unit with a unique network identity, following a protocol that may be utilized by an individual person or a collection of individuals. An agent is defined by reference to membership of a network, and the rights they gain from and give to such a network much the way a 'citizen' is defined by reference to membership of a polity.[68] Through an agent, individuals can collectively relate in ways of their own design (the agent can be itself a network), but when the agent relates to the larger network of which it is one part (a network of networks), it does so with a singular identity and with the capacities of a single economic agent. The network in aggregate is therefore always a network of networks.

Agents relate to the network via the creation and matching of offers, in basically the way individuals or firms in on-line markets for goods and labor tasks make offers. In the network language, the seller makes an offer and the buyer matches the offer. The word 'match' rather than 'accept' relates to the network process of pairing the two sides of an exchange transaction.[69] The purpose may be a one-off transaction but of more interest is the potential for on-going relations: to engage with other agents in *mutual value creation, mutual investing* and *mutual provision of liquidity*: the three domains that define the postcapitalist token system we are designing. What distinguishes an agent in capitalism from one in a postcapitalist economy is the protocols by which they interact in a network.

Markets[70]

The Economic Space Protocol starts with the social as a design object, and is modeled after a network: it specifies the terms and rules by which agents participate in 'the social' as coherent, networked behaviors. The issuance and matching of offers to a network – the social

---

68 The contrast in both cases is with an individual defined autonomously, outside of social context.
69 Offers and matching are explained in more detail in Chapters 9 and 10.
70 See López J. 'Market offers: Distributed trading protocol.' http://marketoffers.manifold.one

relations between agents through the network – are, in the first instance, exchange relations and in this sense constitute a market. But they are also communication relations and in this sense constitute an economic messaging network. The generic exchange relations are defined in the protocols of commodity,[71] credit, and stake exchange. The generic communication relations defined in the protocol are messaging about what is produced, what is collectively accepted as clearing the credit, and collective investment intentions. These exchange messages are elaborated in Chapter 9.

For a network, market relations are effective for scaling, distribution and interoperability, but agents may also engage in 'subnetwork' interactions that may not rely on markets. These may be 'local' and directly co-operative, and these relations could involve quite innovative financial contracts (such as a gift; ownership which decays to the commons, etc.). These are all design questions. But to scale beyond the local, and be quantifiably recognized by the network-at-large, there must be the adoption of the larger network's units of account.

These relations are not conceived around conventionally-defined market 'structures' of competitive, monopolistic, etc.; nor are they conceived around means-ends strategies of agents understood as optimizing individuals. Rather, these relations are conceived around performances: creative, often cooperative, but always social, acts that embed the potential for future effects and future rewards for the performers.

---

[71] This is the first use of the term 'commodity,' which appears frequently in the following analysis. We define 'commodities' to include all outputs produced for, and recognized by, the network. It is not Marx's use of the term, which associates commodities with capitalist production relations. There, commodity production has two dimensions: it is extractive, in the sense that commodities are produced by the workers and owned by the capitalist, and it is produced so as to be sold for a profit. This latter emphasis gives rise to the term 'commodification,' with more and more facets of social life converted into marketable opportunities for extraction. Our use of the term 'commodity' is more like Staffa (1960) in his book *Production of Commodities by Means of Commodities*. There, commodities are all produced outputs. They are produced for a market, but they are not exchanged for money. This gives space for our proposition that commodities can be produced for the commons (without a price). Similarly, there can be no suggestion that our use of the term commodity is subject to a 'fetishism' of commodities, developed by Marx (1867) at the end Chapter 1 of Volume I of *Capital*, for this term, too, is capitalist-specific. In many analyses, the political response to fetishism is to take goods and services out of market relations. Our proposal is to change the nature of markets.

3.3 Economic space

Every economic space shares a common economic grammar or value calculus. Each individual economic space is a communication medium, where economic agents express, through offers and matching, participation in the pursuit of a shared network goal. The focus, therefore, is on shared knowledge or 'expression' which, in turn, can be used to continually redesign economic space, making it inherently adaptive in expressing what is valued.

Framed this way, an economic space is expressed in two dimensions: first in market exchanges (the creation and matching of offers), but noting that the interactions of exchange may not be motivated by either prices nor optimisation strategies; and secondly through performances, where agents take a position on their own and other agent's proposals for future value creation. The focus here is an inter-temporal spread featuring risk, volatility and creativity. In performances it is these dimensions that animate the creation and matching of offers.

3.4 Tokens and distributed ledgers

Ledgers

Ledgers take the form of a digital double entry database; in structure basically no different from a corporate ledger. What will be different is the categories in which ledgers are compiled and the conditions for the entry of quantities against those numbers (the questions of what counts and how it is counted). These will depend on the network's unit of exchange.[72] The network's ledger records multiple instruments/asset types represented in multiple accounts measured in terms of a shared unit of exchange, and thereby made commensurable with any other.

A token system based on distributed ledgers does not require the function of single, universally recognized means of exchange, only that a means of exchange is quantitatively recognisable (has an exchange rate; is commensurable) across a network, where ownership and valuation can be recorded on a verifiable ledger. The reach of any token comes from the extent of a network of ledger relations. Moreover, there need be no presumption that the one token type performs all the 'standard' money functions. Different money functions can be implemented

---

72 The formal explanation of a unit of exchange is developed in Chapter 7.

through different protocols, and different token types can be better or worse at them.[73]

How agents share the data stored on the network ledger is a matter of protocol design. Individual agent data is defined as private, but aggregated data forms the basis of a data commons, in which individual agents may choose their degree of participation.

Tokens

Tokens have many attributes, and those attributes are being introduced at different stages of the analysis. We first introduced tokens in a preliminary way in Chapter 1.4 and in Chapters 9 and 10 they will be given full development. In the current context, we focus on their role in market exchange in the Economic Space Protocol.

Tokens are tickets that signal rights. Formally, fiat money is a subset of tokens[74] and some crypto-tokens, most notably bitcoin, stand with fiat money as a centrally-issued (though distributedly verified) token system. In the Economic Space Protocol, tokens are bearer (smart) contracts, and can express a multitude of modes of instruction. For example, some tokens are more akin to entry tickets (to a bus, concert, etc.) which have a particular use: they are issued by agents and once they have been used, they cannot be reused. Others may be used for clearing of credit, a process explained in Chapter 8. Yet others may be utilized to receive a stream of dividends.

In the new economic space a token is an exclusive, quantifiable set of rights, whose transfer is recorded on and enforced through a ledger. The state of the token is always reflected in the accounting derived from the ledger. When an offer is made by one agent and matched by another (for example for exchange of a commodity), the receipt of the commodity triggers the issuance of a token by the agent who matched the offer; recording the completion of the transaction. So it is individual agents, not a central authority who issues tokens. Some tokens may be redeemed, and become inactive.

Immediately we see that these tokens are not what is popularly thought to be 'money' or 'coins.' They are neither being 'minted' (an operation applicable to 'coins'; not to bearer contracts) or exclusively issued by privileged

---

73 This issue is explored in Chapter 10.
74 The term 'chartalism' to describe state-issuance of money comes from the Latin 'charta,' meaning 'ticket' or 'token'; indicating that money is a type of token.

third parties (as applies with fiat currencies). Hence tokens are not, in themselves, a preferred or agreed upon store of value: a token must always attach to (stand for) a 'real' asset (encoded as a set of contractual rights). A more precise concept is 'material underlier' and there must be 'real' asset transfers associated with token exchanges.[75] For example, wealth may be stored as stake, and recorded by a token entry in the network ledger to that effect (an asset recorded in a ledger as X stake tokens).

In the light of this clarification of tokens, an economic space, as defined in Chapter 3.3, can be respecified as a network where every agent participates in the distribution of tokens, exchanging offers, and archiving those interactions on a verifiable record.

3.5 Ways of 'pricing'

In Chapter 2 we developed a critique of the Hayekian focus on prices and the propensity to reduce all information to a single index. Our counter-proposal was the need to preserve the complexity of information, for it may well find new meaning (form into new performances and new outputs) over time.

In the Economic Space Protocol, an act of exchange registers a transfer of title (ownership), and that transfer will be recorded at a 'price,' in the sense that an object of ledger transfer is attributed a rate of exchange. Our analysis must describe the formation of that quantity, but for now we invoke the idea that an output finds validation (is attributed with value) in the network. The word 'price' is a word that has a popular meaning akin to the way it is used by Hayek, but it is a term we should not surrender to that specific meaning. To reclaim the word we introduce four different notions of 'price':

- A *direct price*. This is a price determined in point-in-time exchange between the agent and the network (ultimately another agent) for a quantum of tokens in an open market. This is somewhat parallel to that found in Hayek, with the additional information dimensions.
- An *indirect price*. This is a price that emerges on the network over time. This will be found for outputs that find no direct price but become

---

[75] In the terminology of Gurley and Shaw (1960) third party issued monies like fiat currency and bitcoin are 'outside money.' Outside money may certainly enter the new economic space, but it will do so as a commodity for exchange. A transfer of outside money within the network will be matched by a token transfer, as it is for any commodity exchange.

inputs into other outputs that do find a direct price. Here is where the maintenance of a chain of information is critical. By following a chain of output-becoming-inputs-becoming-outputs to a point where a direct price is found, the network can retrospectively attribute a share of that direct price to formerly-unpriced inputs back down the chain (see Appendix 4.2).

- A *tribute*. Some right transfers will fit the category of a gift. These could be between individual agents but, most critically for the Economic Space Protocol, these may be gifts to the commons (see Chapter 6.3). The counter-gift is access to the commons, on terms at the discretion of the commons.
- A *synthetic price*. This is a price which can be created by the network to account for outputs which are consumed collectively, most notably those given as tribute. The formula for a synthetic price is (socially validated) costs of production + the average rate of return for the network. Some outputs in the network can be said to produce value (they are socially valued) but they are not designed to be sold. When the network wants to value these (for example in calculating total output of the network) it may invoke a synthetic price.

Indirect prices, tributes and synthetic prices have no parallel in Hayek. They are the forms of price that link most to the process of staking performances

3.6 Peer-to-peer; decentralized to distributed

Economic relations can be thought of as hierarchical or distributed. Hierarchical relations may be centralized (at the top of the pyramid) or decentralized (pushed down the pyramid, for example to regions or sectors or lower down the hierarchy to towns or workplaces). There are also different forms of vertical communication.[76]

We should also distinguish decentralized from distributed. When decision making is decentralized, it is nonetheless part of a hierarchical system. 'Distributed' is defined without reference to hierarchy: all agents have the same formal capacities. In the Economic Space Protocol

---

76 Hayek and indeed all 'neoliberal' economics advocates decentralized markets, with some conditions of 'market failure' and exceptional use of an active centralized agent. Hayek wanted the money used in exchange to be decentralized; the neoclassicals want it centralized.

it means that there is one grammar in the network that every agent can speak, but no central authority: not even a virtual one.

In relation to 'money,' centralized money issuance and centralized clearing divides agents in the network in two classes: those that can issue/clear money, and those that cannot. In the Economic Space Protocol all agents are peers who have the capacity to issue and clear without need for the service of specialized third parties.

Centralized architectures are optimal for mediums that propagate and process information slowly, and hence must maintain information locally. But they scale poorly, as the capacity to react to information, and back-propagate it, becomes increasingly slow as the network grows. High speed communications and information processing media make centralized networking architecture obsolete. It is now possible to distribute to individual agents roles with high information requirements.

3.7 Social objectives

Two issues can be framed here: how agents behave and how collective agendas are expressed in the Economic Space Protocol.

Agents and their goals

Just as the engineering requirements of a network mean starting the analysis with exchange, so there is the requirement of starting with individual agents. The Economic Space Protocol designs the infrastructure through which these agents express their sociality but without a central agent imposing specific social goals. These are process-oriented protocols; not an ends-means system.

The Economic Space Protocol is designed to endow individual agents with a diversity of goals and provide them with capacity to generate a range of modes of measurement of their performances. Agents can pursue goals of their own choosing and measure in ways of their own choosing, but the value proposition of the network means that their success in achieving those goals must be validated by other agents. Sociability is therefore centered on addressing the question of 'what constitutes network 'value,' and how are the rewards for value creation shared across the network?

The dynamic of agents pursuing their own economic vision, but needing to reconcile that vision with collective valuation, is what drives the network. As visions change, and as collective valuation changes, the system embeds a volatility of social expression. In this context, volatility isn't something to fear or eradicate: it is the expression of social development, and opens the space for financial representation of evolving social goals (volatility as a financial spread).

The protocols of the relationship between the individual agent and the system of collective valuation is therefore key to the economic expression of sociability. Posed in simple terms, to be elaborated in later chapters, agents 'invest' in their goals, emotionally, politically and financially, by the performances they choose to undertake and by staking the performances of other agents they believe contribute social value. Investing agents not only diversify their stake holdings (sharing risk) but, with a liquid stake market, staking becomes the network's mode of voting on values see (Chapter 5.2). The on-going preparedness of agents to *keep* staking performances with certain value profiles then starts to define the network's on-going depiction of value.

The collective

The Economic Space Protocol starts with the network as a construct-in-itself: a set of protocols that must be followed by every individual agent who joins the network. It cannot be simply 'assumed-to-exist,' nor does it implicitly take on the social order in which it operates, for social relations are a design choice and agents explicitly must agree to the protocols. But 'the social' cannot be expressed simply as the sum of those individual interactions: it exists at a different level of sociality.

This framing is critical to the new economic space, and warrants brief reflection. The analytical foundation of protocol design is generally individual agents who interact. Protocol design involves the building out of these interactions. But if we think of an economy as a whole, it is more than the sum of these interactions: It is not just a distinction of scale, but also of design too.

There are three critical factors here that are central to understanding *the network premium*, i.e. that the whole as more than simply the sum of individual interactions:

- *The Commons.* There is a need to identify, preserve and expand performances that make collective contributions that are not readily divisible to individual ownership. Protocol design can generate a systematic expansion of the Commons (see Chapter 6).

- *Valuing collective performances.* Some outputs won't be sold, even though they may give social benefit. In a system centered on profit, that means they cannot be counted. But with diverse modes of measuring, selling is not the condition of creating new value.
- *Network performances.* The new economic space is a network of interactions between subnetworks. Each of these subnetworks, and the aggregate network, can be seen as expressing distinct performances in their own right. That is, they are not merely the aggregation of agent performances inside 'their' network: they have distinctive meaning in combination. The overall performance of the new economic space, accordingly, has a meaning that is more than just adding up the individual parts. In particular, the overall performance will reveal the health of the network, partly by reference to data on the mechanics of the protocol and partly as a measure of the success of the network in meeting its (diverse) goals.

3.8 Governance

The Economic Space Protocol constitutes a process of governance through the design of markets and the rights of all individual agents in relation to those markets and hence to other agents. As we clarify these rights in specific applications to the Economic Space Protocol it will become apparent that they lie behind the logic of token issuance (and clearance): rights to issue, create, share and stake in performances, create and receive credit, or exchange commodities.

But the new economy, indeed any economy, needs means to set a collective social agenda; to determine what is valuable is to set priorities which will drive market incentives. This agenda *could* be set by decree from a central authority, or it could be set in a distributed way by markets designed so as to elicit support for possible social agendas. This would make governance of the network the role of all participating agents.

Distributed governance is also critical within production processes, or 'performances' as we call them (see Chapter 4). Each act of valuation/ realignment is a form of decision-making. Unlike voting, which seeks to define a collective making a decision on what to perform, a performance is itself a decision seeking a collective to affirm it. Moreover, valuing performances follows market dynamics. It does not require creating a higher-powered agent like a board that coalesces preferences into discrete events and chooses a majority over a minority. Instead, distributed governance integrates opinions, preferences, and agendas by mutually empowering participants.[77]

In distributed governance, and in the absence of a state as the source of trust in economic processes and institutions, trust must be founded within the network. There are four primary dimensions of this trust:

- trust in the integrity of the network.
- trust in the measurement device.
- trust in the quality and authenticity of what is being measured.
- trust in the counterparty (their risk of non-delivery or default).

In the new economic space, trust in the network depends on trust in the protocol plus trust in participants in the network. The recording of transactions on a distributed ledger, where both seller and buyer confirm completion shifts issues of trust towards the protocol level to ensure that computation is correct, distributed state is consistent, and information is secure, to avoid issues like the 'double spend.' Knowing an agent's transaction histories adds the dimension of a reputation rating for other agents.

Trust in measurement devices and the quality of measurement is the subject of token design, addressed in Chapter 11. The critical issues here are the clear connection of token relations to economic relations, giving tokens a material basis in 'real,' and sustainable economic relations of investing (staking), credit and trade.

3.9 The tools to reframe

This chapter has introduced the core categories of the Economic Space Protocol, and has been designed to meet some specific challenges set out at the start of the chapter.

The consideration of markets in the context of new ways of measuring opens the possibility that things currently deemed desirable but unprofitable – for example care, art, research, affect, biosphere enhancement – can come to prominence as value-creating activities. They need not be seen as after-thoughts, to be 'subsidized' by the state or private philanthropists because they are virtuous-but-unprofitable.

---

77 The effect is a distributed *economic intellect*, referring to Marx's notion of the *general intellect*, which in its turn refers to the final phase of capitalism, where capital itself generates the seed of its destruction when knowledge and social powers of interaction replace direct labor and labor time at the core of the production of wealth. See Virtanen (2006).

The distributed nature of economic spaces focuses on the capacities of individual agents to pursue their own goals of value creation, to make offers to the network, to issue tokens, to reciprocally stake and, as we will see in later chapters, to issue credit. But the Economic Space Protocol is always drawing these individual agendas back to their social meanings and collective validation. This is framed not as a constraint on individual expression but as the condition for sociability; indeed, the condition for having a sense of the collective social agenda (network health, the commons, etc.) that is beyond the capacity of agents conceived as just an aggregation of individuals, to achieve.

The concepts and categories introduced in this chapter provide us with the tools we need for Economic Space Protocol design. In subsequent chapters these concepts and categories, and the way they combine together, will be explained and scrutinized in greater detail.

CHAPTER 4

PRODUCTION AS PERFORMANCE

4.1 Background

Chapter 3 presents the conceptual categories of exchange that serve as the foundation of performances. This chapter outlines the general nature of performances. It links closely with the following chapter on stake, which engages the way in which performances are valued by the network.

Performances must also be understood as protocols of a network. This is a process of recognising performances as a sequence of events, making them both composable and divisible, so that they can be encoded (see Chapter 4.3). They are also interactive: across the network, they must be perceived, communicated and enacted. So each performance always includes an offer to the network, describing its organization, proposed outputs, proposed outcomes of those outputs, how their value should be measured, token issuance, governance, surplus distribution, etc.. Performances thus have scripts – to 'perform' the sequence of events – and are to be understood as expressions to be evaluated by the network.

A performance is akin to what economics calls 'production,' but we utilize the broader term for the following reasons:

- 'Performance' puts the emphasis on creativity and innovation of those performing, unlike 'production' which is often associated with the repetitive discipline of a production line.
- How a performance is designed and implemented is determined by the performers, unlike production which is often associated with hierarchical control.
- A performance has an audience; production has a market. An audience may pay directly to consume/participate, but it may not. Part of the innovation of the new economic space is the recognition that contri-

butions to value can take multiple forms: they won't all be expressed through direct exchange in a market.
- It follows that there must be mechanisms of social (audience) acknowledgment and verification that value is being created. The returns to performers that come from a social acknowledgment of value creation are determined by relations of staking between agents, not extractive relations of wage labor and capital.

So performances express what makes a postcapitalist economy a different experience for those participating in it: it places their creativity and their intention to create social meaning at the center of the economy and scripts them as offers to the network. It is then up to the network to determine whether these proposals warrant support by staking. Here is where the diversity of values, and different modes of measuring value, take on practical meaning, both in agents' decisions about what to produce and how to produce it, but also in their claims to create value for the network.

4.2 Performing relations

In the Hayekian (and neoclassical) framing of markets, there is no analysis of the process of production of outputs. There are inputs of labor, materials and technology, all acquired by exchange, and there are outputs sold for money. So there is an account for what goes into production and what comes out, but what goes on inside the production process is unexplained. Marx was decisively different in this regard. Marx depicts the relations in the process of production as the defining feature of a capitalist economy. It is the domain of the owners of the means of production (the employer of labor). The workplace runs at their discretion and wage workers must comply, subject to some degree of legally-imposed standards. These are the social relations Marx depicted as extractive: where workers produce more net output value than their wages can purchase. They produce a surplus, belonging to the owner.

In a postcapitalist economy we need a different analysis of the organization of performances. The contemporary literature on postcapitalism focuses heavily on democratic workplace relations, flat hierarchies and workers' control over production decisions. In the light of the disturbing histories of 20th century centrally-controlled 'socialist' states, current proposals for postcapitalist priorities tend to gravitate to the virtue of direct p2p, community modes of organization, most of which are not designed to scale.

The protocols of the new economic space remain silent on the social relations of each performance. There are no standards or norms about how each performance may be defined and executed, how decisions are made, what metrics get generated and how performance revenues are shared between internal participants. In a distributed system it is the performance participants[78] who must determine the social relations of that performance and associated governance structure. However, although those 'performing relations' are determined by participants, they are nonetheless subject to network scrutiny. Performing relations are themselves a performance offer to the network, and subject to network evaluation in the same way other performance proposals are subject to network evaluation. We might anticipate that the social relations of a performance will be a critical issue for prospective stakers (and stakers of stakers). These relations can, thereby, be a site of continuing improvement, for that improvement is itself a claim to value creation.

4.3 Protocols of performances[79]

A performance is the organization of a coherent set of actions across a network to achieve a stated goal as a network state change. It must be recognized by agents in the network as constituting a discrete series of events. Socially and culturally, a performance offer is an expression of an intention to create something of social worth and have it recognized and verified by the network; in effect, to be declared as value.

The term 'recognition' is important here, and it must have a formal meaning, for while a performance may be depicted as a creative, expressive offer, it must also be ledger-compatible. As defined by the International Financial Reporting Standards (IFRS Foundation 2015:12) 'recognition is the process of capturing an asset or liability for inclusion in the financial statements.' So it links closely to the chosen units in which a financial account is compiled and presented (see Chapter 7). Suffice it here

---

78 Stakers could, for this purpose, be considered participants. They could make their staking conditional on the performance offer having a certain structure, including its social relations in production. Furthermore, we expect performing relations to become a new value layer: a critical performance outcome.

79 See López, J. 'Network Performance: Distributed Computing Protocol.' http://network-performance.manifold.one

to say that recognition relates to the way a creative offer is expressed to the network in a way the network will recognise as a proposal to create a new asset.

Financially, a performance implies taking on a risk position on the future: a calculation that the costs of mounting a performance will generate new value in excess of those costs (a surplus in some form). Performances will generally be intentionally planned, but it is possible that network data may reveal the conditions of an 'unplanned' performance.

Performances may be 'closed' or 'open' (or have recognizable dimensions of each), reflecting distinctive risk positions:

- A *closed performance*. This is a pre-scripted process with a determinate end. It may be thought of as a one-off or a defined series. The quantification of outputs here is relatively straightforward and the risk is associated with the costs relative to Value creation of a broadly-known output.
- An *open performance*. Where the stated goal is aspirational and the performance may not have a clear beginning, nor a clear end, it is called an open-ended performance. Its outputs are likely to be inputs for 'higher-order' performances, just as its own inputs will likely be combinations of other, 'lower-order' performances. The implied complexity and coordination makes the pricing of outputs and of stake more about broader, collective, network goals than individual ones (see Appendix 4.2). It is likely that performances offered to the commons will be open rather than closed performances.

In elaborating the nature of performances there are concepts that we will first define separately, and then bring together:

- *Information: any performance-related data recorded in the network.*[80] The network will 'automatically' create the possibility of recording a vast range of data. These will most obviously be about times, places and prices of exchange, but there can readily be produced adjunct data. These could be about performance scripts, design and execution, the agents and their trading histories, time intervals between offers and network matching, intensities of interest from other agents, agent

---

80 The network holds all records, of which the ledger is just one type; for example, records of offers made, even if they do not get a match. Moreover, it warrants emphasizing that it is performances that encode information with meaning.

satisfaction, networks of connection between exchanging agents, state changes in the project organization, bits transferred, documents created, and more.
- *Event: sets of data thought to have a combined meaning (a data narrative).* Data analytics could readily be built on top of these raw data. The simplest analytic we call an *economic event*: the identification of data happening in combinations (a+b)[81] where a and b could be raw data or themselves compiled from statistical analytics. One can imagine a tree of a's and b's combining to form new, 'higher-order' a's and new b's.
- *Events in combinations: events (data narratives) which can cause desired effects.* Events are devoid of a causal proposition over time. But when we propose causality (a+b leads to c), we invoke the conditions for a performance. Events in combinations may then be treated as higher-order events themselves. When data are encoded as narratives, they adopt the grammar of value, but still lack the verification of the network that is the condition of value.
- *Performance: innovation and risk.* Events in combinations propose causality, but no innovation. So if the proposition a+b leads to c were posed in the subjunctive tense – if a+b *were to* lead to c – we add a contingency, for a+b may or may not lead to c. The subjunctive proposition becomes a risk exposure when the occurrence of c has consequences which can be expressed financially. This is a performance in the domain of taking a position on the future: a performance, framed in the subjunctive, with financial consequences.
- *Performance index: measuring the execution of a performance.* This is a specific calculation on the information produced by the technical data on performance (it is the result of a mathematical formula). It has a magnitude that is expected to change over time. It also has a type, which is the particular dimension of quantifiable measurement (e.g. transaction speed, liquidity index, average transaction volume, carbon footprint, engagement index) that makes all performances commensurable in these dimensions.
- A *measurement of value: network responses to a performance.* This involves the identification of whether a performance has met its verifiable outcome targets (measures of social effects) sufficient to be validated by the network as the creation of value. No measure can

---

81 By '+' in this context we mean simply 'in combination with,' where combinations may be expressed in any way that is deemed to have economic significance.

be made until the completion of a first performance, but this measurement serves as information for staking on second and subsequent performances.
- *Stake: network calculation of future performances.* This results from the preparedness to invest in some ownership of a performance. Stake frames contingency as potentiality. It takes the contractual form: 'I am prepared to stake an asset in expectation of a yield, should future events occur.' All the above data can impact decisions to stake a performance, but most obviously the performance index and the measurement of value.

We can now see these dimensions in combination. The information generation that is triggered around an act of exchange and the enactment of a performance can be framed as the basis for individual agents to take positions on the performance or consequences of the economic endeavor. With slight elaboration, we identify the codification of data into performances whose contingency can be staked. A critical proposition follows. Something produced with potential, measurable social significance – be it a physical good, a service, or an intangible – could be offered to the network. It is expressed socially as a performance, qualitatively as a measurement of value, quantitatively as a performance index and made investable as a stake.

4.4 Performance Indices and value measures

Any agent can transform information into an index or 'measure' and publish it to the market, but whether it becomes network-recognized will depend on others adopting it to measure their activities consistent with its meaning. An index or other measure must be endorsed by the network and in this sense, indices have attributes of produced commodities: they are themselves 'performed.'

Performance indices

These measure performances of technical processes of output creation. They are the mode of measuring (counting) outputs of a performance. Quantification is critical in any economy, but in the Economic Space Protocol these quantities are not immediately or always converted to a universal unit of exchange (prices and revenues). The compilation of indices must preserve how output and outcome qualities are different-but-measurable.

Performance indexes measure combinations of data that seek to capture statistical relations designed to depict events, using nominated measures such as repetitions, influence, replications and attraction. A performance could be a single event-with-consequences (e.g. other performances reference/adopt/adapt this performance) or the event is itself repeated, with each repeat triggering recognition. Either way, it involves the identification and quantification of a continuous set of indicators, that are defined at the time the performance is offered for stake. Quantifying occurrences makes different outputs quantitatively commensurable (as a spread), without reducing them to a single measure. Notice that this framing preserves the diversity of measures to preclude them being reduced to a single index (which would then look like a conventional price). In summary, performance indices preserve what is qualitatively distinctive about outputs and outcomes while at the same time counting their occurrences (quantifying).

Value measures

These identify performances as expressive acts of productive creation, designed to produce value for the network. A performance starts as an agent making an offer to the network. That offer must specify how the performance will be undertaken, the outputs of the performance, and the intended social outcomes of those outputs It is on the basis of this offer – the proposed performance and its nominated mode of network recognition – that other agents in the network will decide whether, and to what extent, they will stake the performance. The mechanics of this process are developed in Appendix 4.1 and in Chapter 7.

Each performance is therefore valued in the network to reflect two things:

- *The worth of the performance.* Is the performance recognized by the network as an expression of its determination of what constitutes value creation?; are there good, clear measures?; will the specified 'indexification' provide an effective measure of the performance goal? For example, for a performance related to human care, the network will be determining whether the way care is defined in an offer, how the provision of care is organized and managed, and the way units of care performance are specified (e.g. recipient responses; physical wellbeing of the recipient, etc.) are considered stakeable, and at what stake price?

- *The 'pricing' of outputs of the performance.* This relates to the four modes identified in Chapter 3.5. This pricing process – ranging from direct sale to tributes to the commons – will see the network's valuation of the outputs of a performance.

4.5 A 'value theory of performance'

In our analysis we refer many times to 'value,' and do so not simply in an ethical sense of what is deemed desirable, but also in a technical economic sense of being a way of measuring. So what do we mean by this latter meaning of 'value'? Broadly speaking, in economics there are two types of value theories.

One is based on 'objective' measures that sit outside of market prices. The most prevalent are labor theories of value of which Marx's is the best known.[82] Value in this approach is related to labor time embedded directly or indirectly in a produced commodity. What makes this a social theory is that all different sorts of labor are conceptually convertible to units of abstract labor: that which all acts of labor share in common. When we frame that as a relation to capital and production for profit, all labor stands collectively as the creators of output and capital collectively as the owners of the output.

The other type of value theory adopts 'subjective' measures that are focussed directly on the individual preferences of sellers and buyers and how they interact in a market, to exchange at a price. Broadly this covers neo-classical and Hayekian approaches. The social dimension here (which might constitute an approach to 'value') is the way that all individuals' preferences combine to form prices that clear markets, in a process gravitating to equilibrium (neoclassical) or spontaneous order (Hayekian). The socialness is that as each agent changes their decision, it impacts on price, and hence on the decisions of every other agent.

Most adherents of this latter approach, however, would not generally describe themselves as 'value theorists,' for they recognize no domain of calculation other than price. Conversely, for those who adhere to 'objective' theories of value, price is real, but superficial: value defined in the

---

82 Sraffa (1960) proposes a Marx-compatible approach to value that is not centered on labor time. We admire this work as opening a way of framing value in a postcapitalist economy. In acknowledging Sraffa, we might call our own approach 'production of performances by means of performances.'

realm of production is the long-term driver of markets, and prices are a response to short-term factors, but will tend to vary around longer-term (labor) values.

The Economic Space Protocol draws on both, but complies with neither of these theories of value.

Labor-based approaches to value were designed to explain the workings of capitalism, not the conditions for postcapitalism. Indeed, in the domain of social relations of performance defined by staking and innovation, it is social effects, not labor inputs that will be the key to value. For the Economic Space Protocol, value relates to the social recognition (staking) of the performance itself; not social recognition (purchase) of the outputs of performances. The difference is subtle, but significant.

Labor-based approaches struggle to deal with the 'value' of outputs where marginal costs are virtually zero. This problem was originally posed in this sort of value theory as the difficulty of putting a value on nature. Nature, being created without labor, could be treated as the exception. But today, intangible outputs like software, networks and knowledge are increasingly prevalent in the economy, but labor time in production seems to explain very little.[83] Our depiction of performances associated with exchange is designed precisely to account for the collective contribution of intangibles in new, creative ways.

A subjective preference approach to value, conversely, faces no such challenge from intangibles, but price has to be framed around private patent ownership and contrived scarcity. Software markets reach a clearing price, but only by social exclusion (e.g. by restricting access; hiding the source code). So recognition of intangibles in this approach can only be achieved by a private, not an innately social, approach to value.

A postcapitalist approach to value must encode ways to value the social that are not expressed via quantified labor, nor simply by output price. Indeed, there should be no suggestion that price and value are, or can be made, of the same quantities: a proposition that haunts Marxian value theory (the problem of 'transforming' values defined in socially necessary labor time into (smoothed) prices). In our analysis, value comes from the attribution of social recognition, and we will later identify how this recognition might be measured, but these are not proxy prices. The 'conver-

---

83 The proposition is not that labor theories of value cannot explain intangibles like software, for the labor of the software designer could indeed be counted. It is that little about the significance of software in value formation is going to be explained by this attribution.

sion' from values to prices, if there is indeed such a process, is expressed through staking: how agents change their staking decisions in response to value measures, but it is a tendency only; not a formal connection. This is why we focus on the *performance as the mode of expression* of value. A performance may be initiated by an exchange in a market but, in contrast with subjective preference approaches, it is the social meaning that can be built around the exchange, not the exchange itself, that is critical to value creation. Moreover, and unlike 'objective' approaches to value, the goal is not to explain each commodity's value in terms of output metrics, but to identify a network perspective on what outputs are deemed to create value for the network: how a producing population of agents creates, funds and maintains collective benefits for the network.

To achieve this focus, we must look at the social consequences of production and exchange. To say that an output is a social contribution, it is not sufficient to say that it sells for a price, nor that it was produced by labor for the market,[84] but that it is validated by the protocols of the network (see Appendix 4.1 and Chapter 7).

For this to be impactful on the growth of the economy, and on incentives for producing agents, there must be trailing commissions, yields or dividends attributable to performers and other owners of stake in the performance. This is why postcapitalism must link to stake: the skin in the game that holds the connection between initial production and collective benefit (or, indeed, cost).

Performance is the mode of expression of value that runs through from an initiating act, triggered by exchange, to broader social consequences. We could, therefore, call this a 'performance theory of value.' But, following Elson (1979) on Marx's value theory, we prefer to depict it as a *'value theory of performance.'* Our goal is not to use individual performances to explain value, but to use the social conditions of value to give meaning to individual performances.

---

84 We are aware of Marx's concept of *socially necessary* labor time, making acceptance of a commodity in the market a condition of value. The point here is consistent with that condition of value.

APPENDIX 4.1

A PERFORMANCE EVALUATION FRAMEWORK

Chapter 4.4 identified the dual measurements of performance indices and value measurement. While noting in Chapter 4.5 that these are not competing modes of measuring the same thing, how they relate together warrants explanation. That explanation requires other elements, such as staking (Chapter 5) and so will be clarified in Chapter 7 on postcapitalist modes of measurement. In the current context of performances, we can identify public policy initiatives, associated originally with the British (HM) Treasury, that address the measurement of social impacts in a way that directly parallel the processes we are invoking, and which have been critical in framing our analysis.[85]

Social impact bonds

These are sometimes called social benefit bonds or pay-for-success bonds.[86] They were first implemented by the British state in 2010 to fund social policy expenditures on experimental projects. These were initially programs to address prisoner recidivism and then programs for family reunification in the context of children taken into the state's welfare system. Around the world, there have since been many other applications.

The critical innovation of social impact bonds is that they design a bond for a private investor to purchase, where the funds raised from the bond sale are spent on an experimental public policy intervention (i.e. where the outcome is unknown). The intervention must be undertaken by an 'independent' third party, not a party to the contract, to ensure the results are verifiable. The bet for the investor is whether the intervention will achieve a pre-specified level of success (if, for example, a group of

---

[85] We acknowledge here the contribution of Pamela Hansford who brought this literature to our attention and advised on its application.

[86] Social impact bonds are said to have been first invented by a New Zealand economist Ronnie Horesh in 1988.

prisoners that receives the intervention has 20% lower rate of recidivism than a control group). If the intervention is successful in achieving its 20% target, the investors get a payout; if not, they lose their money.[87]

This innovation had two relevant features for our purpose. First, the design of social impact bonds embeds the criteria by which success (an investor payout) would be verified. This is not a policy of 'intervene first and evaluate after': the conditions of evaluation (the 20% improvement condition, for example) is known to the investor before they invest. In the depiction of performances presented in this chapter, this is an important feature: the performance offer must declare its claims to independently verifiable outcomes, and the probability of these targeted levels being achieved enters into investor calculation about staking the performance. In a social impact bond, independent verifiability is undertaken by a separate institution: neither the state nor the investor, but the third party commissioned to undertake the intervention. In the new economic space, it is believed that network-generated data will be the primary source of independent verification. However, an agent could offer the performance of verification services to the network.

Second, the design of social impact bonds enables the quantification of social phenomena generally thought unmeasurable. It measures not an absolute outcome (what number (to appear on a ledger) could be given to a successful recidivism reduction program, and what is the measure of 'success'?) but the spread between the intervention group and the control group (was there a 20 percent difference?). This spread is the objective of calculation. If the intervention achieves a 20 percent spread, the intervention is deemed successful and the investor gets an agreed bond payout; if not, the investors lose their money.[88] This closes the intervention: the investor has received payment (or not) and the state has discovered whether the intervention is worth permanent funding (or not).

The lesson for the new economic space is that measurement of performance outcomes, as the condition for declaring value, will be found in the design and pricing of spreads. This is a framing in the logic of financial derivatives: pricing the spread on the performance of an asset rather

---

87 In practice, the investors do not lose all their money. Governments' desires to promote the policy have tended to set generous terms for investors.

88 Social impact bonds involve the government funding an experimental intervention to determine whether it should receive on-going state funding. They were never designed to be on-going modes of service provision, for a repeat of the same intervention involves no calculation of investor risk, and hence no rationale for investor return.

than pricing the value of the underlying asset itself. The financial derivative framing is developed in Appendix 5.2; the mode of measurement itself in addressed in Chapter 7.3

Policy evaluation framework

The second critical policy development of HM Treasury is the *Magenta Book: Central Government Guidance on Evaluation* (2020), first published in 2011, now extended and elaborated. Its framework has been adopted and adapted by many states' treasuries as the foundation for their policy evaluation frameworks. In our terms, it addresses directly the question of how value gets attributed to the outcomes of a performance, including when these outputs that generate the outcomes are not sold.

The Magenta Book adopts some of the analytical insights of social impact bonds, but gives them a more general context. It is designed, as the subtitle suggests, to give guidelines for policy evaluation generally: an agenda that implicitly includes means to commensurate the value created by different policies.

It is not the purpose of this appendix to summarize that extensive document, but to highlight two important features that are germane to the new economy space and the Economic Space Protocol. First, as with social impact bonds, the *Magenta Book* proposes knowing the method of evaluation before the policy commences; indeed designing the policy *so as to be* measurable. Second, it advocates drawing a difference between outputs and outcomes. Outputs are generally easy to quantify: number of reports or recommendations, surveys conducted, dollars spent, tonnes of this; hours of that, etc.. But outputs are not ends in themselves. It is on outcomes that policy aspires to exert an impact, and outcomes have to be measured differently from outputs,[89] often via the 'spread method' developed in social impact bonds.

The relevance to the Economic Space Protocol is that performances create *outputs* (goods, services, etc.) and performance indices can measure the technical, data attributes of these outputs, giving them a technical point of comparison like transaction speed and volumes. But these are not the point of access to a determination of an individual value and the commensuration of different values. What the *Magenta Book* empha-

---

89 The questions of how, when and how often to measure outcomes have become big questions in public sector use of the evaluation framework, as they will be in a new economic space.

sizes in a policy context is that the critical task is to measure the *outcomes* of outputs. In the new economic space, the measure of outcomes is the equivalent to the process by which the network attributes value to the outputs of a performance. It is asking the question of whether a performance output led to the creation of something of value. Outcomes are the way in which the network will recognize (in the sense defined in Chapter 4.3) a performance's value. This reinforces the emphasis, in both social impact bonds and public policy design, that outcome measures are embedded in the design of performance offers.

APPENDIX 4.2

PERFORMANCES (P) AND THEIR OUTPUTS (C)

Production can be depicted diagrammatically as the relation between performances (P) and commodity outputs (C). By the term 'commodity' to reiterate, we do not mean something produced by wage labor to be sold for a profit (as Marx uses the term) but any good or service that is offered to the network. This appendix includes reference to token types which will not be explained until Chapter 10. Their inclusion here, even at this stage of the analysis, will give the reader some idea of the role tokens play in the network.

Simple commodity production

We start with simple commodity production as a baseline (Figure 4.1) and add complexity.

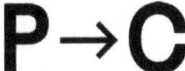

Figure 4.1 Simple commodity production

This is where a single act of 'performance' is directly sold as a commodity. A performance, in this context, equates to an act of production of an output to be offered for sale. This is distinct from an exchange of C – C, where there is a circulation of existing commodities

Cumulative commodity production

Here, performances combine to produce commodities. This may be simply two performances in combination creating a higher level performance (a 2 link chain), which is then realized as a commodity. This 2 link chain is shown in Figure 4.2.

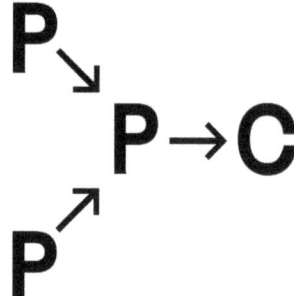

Figure 4.2 Cumulative commodity production

Or it could be more complex chains of performances combining, with different numbers of links (performances) in the chain, such as shown in Figure 4.3.

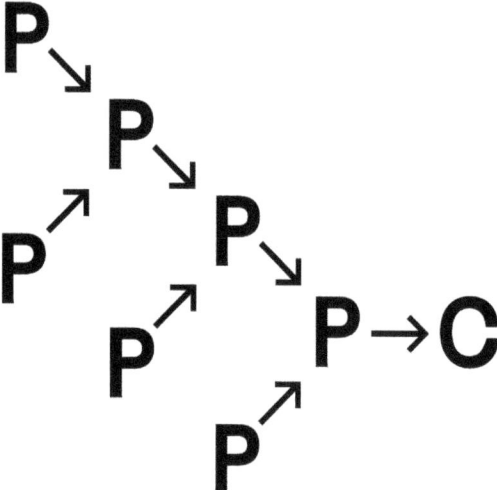

Figure 4.3 Chains of performance

In each above case, a single commodity event occurs (i.e. the performances combine to produce one network unit of value). The production of output is defined by the various performance chains that link to produce a commodity.

The effect of being realized as a commodity valued by the network then triggers claims on that commodity valuation, and a flow of 'revenue' claims in the opposite direction. This occurs by the automated issuance of a commodity token for each recording of a commodity value event in the network. The commodity token is then distributed (into partial shares) back down the performance chain, so that each performance that feeds into a commodity claims a share of Value.

When an agent attributes values to a performance, it does so by 'clearing' or crediting the 'performing agent.' The effect is to validate an exchange of value by issuing a commodity token. For the owner of the performance, this crediting effectively enables them to settle credit, and as credit is held against stake, the net balance of stake increases. Critically, where 'Value' is being recognized in the network not as monetary return (sale for a price) but asset of performances validated by the network, then the 'benefits' of successful performances are revealed not as monetary revenue, but as a reduction in outstanding liquidity: a wealth effect, not an income effect.

Hence, the value of the commodity token is that it is the means by which agents party to the chain of performances can clear credit (which has been issued against stake; see below). How those shares are divided is contractually determined at each link in the chain. When an individual 'P' is many links away from 'C,' its share of the issued commodity token may be relatively small; conversely, an individual 'P' may form a link in many chains, and thus access a share of commodity tokens from many sources.

Further, commodities may combine with performances to create higher-level commodities as depicted in Figure 4.4.

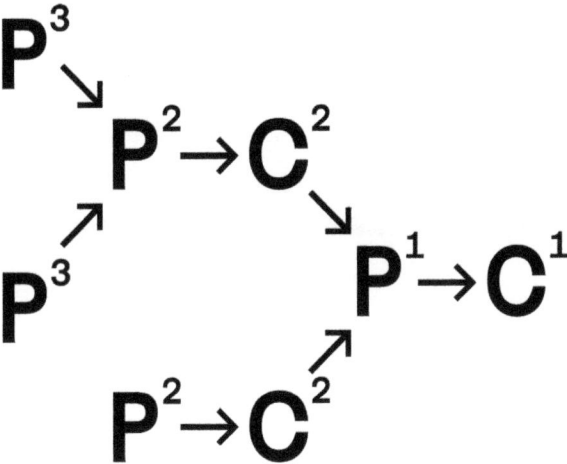

Figure 4.4 Combined performances

Reading from right to left, realization of the value of C1 triggers the issuance of a commodity token and hence a counterflow of liquidity clearing revenue to the owners of P3 in recognition of their contribution to commodity value. When the counterflow reaches C2, the direct benefits accrue to the owner of C2, though the network acknowledgment of the contribution to value of C2 also flows through to the P2 and P3 levels, for their indirect contribution to C1. Each 'level' of claim on the value of C1 is contractually negotiated with the level above. This emphasizes that the conversion of performances (or combinations of performances) into commodities may be seen as the end of a particular performance chain, but new chains may emerge out of commodities, creating more complex commodities. The relation between performances and commodities comes to depict a Leontief-style input-output model.

CHAPTER 5

STAKE: THE KEY TO VALUE

5.1 Introduction

Reciprocal staking involves agents investing in the performances of others by relinquishing stake in themselves. But it is more than simply each agent acquiring a portfolio of assets with diversified risk. Staking is the way in which agents and the network as a whole commit to a future, by backing proposals to create new economic value. Without a pre-specified, external notion of value (e.g. by reference to profit) staking immediately opens an economic and social imaginary of what the priorities of that future could be, both individually and collectively. It gives the network a dynamic of growth, disruption and realignment, and the collective, exploratory choice of direction.

The process of agents in a network taking stake in each others' performances could be subject to a range of economic and social interpretations. Is it a petit bourgeois (small business) stock exchange, with an extractive logic? So does it imply a logic of some agents devouring others and an inevitable polarization of wealth? If posed outside the Economic Space Protocol, this is a possible meaning.

In the context of the Economic Space Protocol, staking points in a different direction, although partial parallels with a capitalist stock exchange should be acknowledged, and the contrasts should be drawn to make the differences stark. (Terminologically, we use the word 'stake' in the Economic Space Protocol and 'stock' in relation to the capitalist stock market.) Four key points of comparison feature prominently in this chapter.

First, unlike the stock market, the market for stake involves *reciprocal* investing. Agents enter the network not with a quantity of money with which to acquire stake in others, nor by offering themselves as wage workers (both of which would then play out an extractive logic of growing wealth inequality), but with proposals for performances or with propensity to participate in others' performances actively and/or financially. We see a shift towards what Marx called 'free association' and individual 'self activity.'[90] The role of the Commons in expressing this propensity towards postcapitalism, is explored in Chapter 6.

Second, the criteria of performance success are different for stock and for stake. In broad terms, in capitalist countries, corporate governance legislation requires making profit to be a priority objective,[91] with just a small amount of wriggle room to enable recognition of so-called social, environmental and governance input (so-called ESGaccounting). In the new economic space, the goals of investors and performances are not pre-specified. We refer here not to the recognition that some investors may be altruistic, and not profit-driven, for that also happens in capitalism. Rather, the network's goals are determined in distributed processes and subject to change according to the changing view of the network.

Third, stock and stake involve different risk allocations. New stake is created and issued as part of a mutual stakeholding transaction. In effect, each party to the transaction, and their respective networks, are underwriting each others' issuance. As stake forms collateral for credit, the parties are also underwriting each others' credit issuance. The intention, as with stock market equity, is to expand net value creation and hence the net value of stake itself. Although new stake issuance 'dilutes' the proportion of total stake held by extant stakeholders, it is associated with an expansion of the performance potential of the underlying assets. The new stake therefore opens a new risk (the expansion) but also a shared risk (the underwriting).

---

90 For Marx, this stage was directly contingent on advanced technology developed in capitalism and involved the proletariat freeing itself of capitalist class relations so that this individual expressiveness and free association could flourish. This technological development and its social conditions Marx referred to the 'force of production' or 'productive forces.' In the words of Marx:

> The appropriation of these forces [of production] is itself nothing more than the development of the individual capacities corresponding to the material instruments of production. The appropriation of a totality of instruments of production is, for this very reason, the development of a totality of capacities in the individuals themselves . . . .
>
> This appropriation is further determined by the manner in which it must be effected through a union . . . . Only at this stage does self-activity coincide with material life, which corresponds with the development of individuals into complete individuals and the casting off of all natural limitations. (Marx 1854, Part 1, Section D)

91 There is nonetheless ambiguity here, especially about how profit is defined and the time horizon for profit maximization.

Fourth, mutual stakeholding transactions are strategic and continual and they convey critical information to the rest of the network. Issued stake quantity, price and transaction data are essential feedback, for they signal network perceptions (current and anticipated future) of the value creation capacities of each performance. Those perceptions about network recognition can change. Agents may seek to realign their stake portfolios by acquiring more stake or they may partially or fully exit a staking relationship. This depiction may also describe the decision-making process of a hedge fund or venture capitalist, but mutual staking makes both the risks and the consequences of staking decisions markedly different.

Behind staking are acts of exchange: in transacting stake, there will be offers and matches recorded on a network ledger.[92] It follows that we are starting to see the conditions for the emergence of tokens as representations of these transactions. However, the consideration of tokens in relation to staking will be delayed until the social relations of staking are explained. This analytical sequence means that, at this stage of the analysis, there is not yet an elaborated unit of exchange in the network (see Chapters 7.2 and 9), so staking, as considered in this chapter, involves the determination only of relative values (ratios or equivalences) and just a conceptual reach to how they might be made operational as absolute values.

5.2 The circular logic of reciprocal staking[93]

The four points of difference between postcapitalist staking and capitalist stock purchasing point to two leading questions of the new economic space: first, how do we understand the rates at which agents will acquire stake in others and give up stake in themselves; and second, if expected profit is not the calculus that motivates staking decisions, what is?

Staking ratios

When agents acquire stake in others by giving up stake in themselves, a critical issue is the decision of how much each invests in the other. Reciprocal staking will not simply involve Agent A acquiring one unit of stake in each of B and C and Agent B one unit of stake in A and C,

---

92 The mechanics of this process are examined in Chapter 10.2.
93 See López, J. 'Market shares: Distributed Staking Protocol.' http://marketshares.manifold.one

etc.. It is the *ratios of allocation* that prove critical: how much stake A must be given up in order to acquire a unit of stake in B may be different from how much A is ready to give up to acquire a unit of stake in C. What these ratios reveal is the network's *relative* view of each agent's past and expected performances: those with the highest ratio (who have received the largest amount in stake offers, relative to others, and whose stake price is rising) are deemed the greatest contributors to value creation (see Chapter 7.3 for the process). The higher your ratio, the more the rest of the network values your performance relative to other performances. Reciprocal staking is the determination of these ratios. The process by which these ratios appear as absolute numbers is not considered until Chapter 8.4, for credit and liquidity are key to this development.

Even though the differences in prices between the stake tokens of different agents are vital to the system's functioning in the short and medium terms, as means of empowering agents proportionally to the perceived value of their performances, they may create imbalances in the long term. Therefore, depending on the nature of the performance, the economic space can introduce inequality mitigation policies. One such policy is stake decay: as the stake held by an agent increases as a determined rate or to a determined level, some part of that stake will start decaying into the network (other stakeholders or the commons), according to a function. Stake decay or other redistribution policies are a design choice for every economic space and something to be considered by agents when deciding to participate.

Decisions to stake other agents' performances

Staking involves investing in the inter-temporal contingencies of individual performances and how they are valued by the network. We can think of it as a sequence of three questions faced by an agent considering proposing a performance of whether to match another agent's staking offer:

- what they would like to see happen in the future.
- what they think is likely to happen in the future.
- how they value what happens in the future and the past.

The first of these – what would be good to happen – is an *aspirational* perspective. It invokes an emotional response to investing. Agents seek to author performances and stake the performances of other agents to generate outputs they would like generated by the network: what they individually think creates 'value.'

The second – what is likely to happen – is a *predictive* perspective. It invokes a calculative response to investing. It involves each agent positioning their own aspirations of performance and staking in the context of expectations of the network as a whole. It invokes a competitive response to investing. Indeed, if this is where our analysis stops, staking would be no more than simply financially positioning on the mood of the market. It would, to invoke Keynes' critique of stock markets, involve placing bets on what other people think will be successful. Keynes' critique is considered directly in Appendix 5.1

The third – interpreting the network's response to performances – is an *evaluative* perspective. It invokes a social response to investing (see Chapter 4.4 and Appendix 4.1). It reveals a network perspective on which performances end up creating value in the network.

This is not a sequence of decisions: each is being made and remade simultaneously, as depicted in Figure 5.1. In capitalism, aspirations may be no different from the new economy, but prediction is about popular opinion about profit and evaluation is dictated by the profit outcomes. In the new economic space, evaluation is not by a predetermined criterion; it is determined by the network. If evaluation is endogenous, then prediction has no singular goal, and hence aspirations can be more expressive. Similarly, if evaluation is a social process, it feeds into emotion, into individual decisions about what to offer to the network and hence also into predictions.

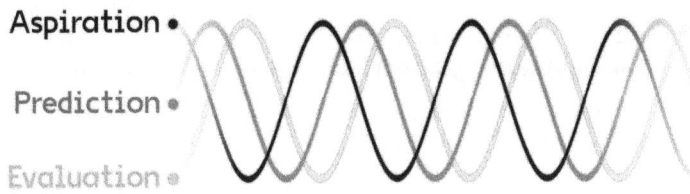

Figure 5.1 Aspirations, Predictions and Evaluations

Endogenous evaluation means that what a network does value can be a mediated expression of what the network aspires to value, so long as there is diversity in predictions. There will be diversity in predictions because agents are not only predicting which individual performances will be successful; they are simultaneously determining the criteria of success.

Most agents, including those pursuing their own explicit maximization strategies, will diversify their predictions because they cannot know in advance the criteria by which their predictions will be evaluated. This process will see agents mining network data seeking investment trends and network opinions. Data analysis will not converge on a single outcome, but it may well see convergence to a range of aspirations, a range of modes of verification (performance indices) and a range of criteria of value. How broad or narrow these ranges are will be played out by the network itself.

Combined

Our consideration of staking ratios involved depicting staking as a voting process in the network: which agents are perceived to be popular to stake and which unpopular. The consideration of the feedback processes in agents' staking decisions shows that staking is more than voting. To invoke the terms of Benjamin Graham (sometimes called the 'Dean of Wall Street' and the father figure of 'value investing') in discussing the stock market, in the short run this market is a voting machine – determining the network's popular views about how each agent's proposal to produce value compares with other agents' proposals – but in the long run it is a weighing machine, evaluating the relative substance of each agent's performances.[94] The weighing mechanism is about collectively determining how much each performance contributes to the network's creation of new value, and hence determining exactly what is meant by a quantity of value (for this particular network).

How can a network measure the value of things even though there may be no single, 'objective' measure of value and, indeed, some output may never be sold for a price? The answer is that the willingness of agents to stake a performance shifts the focus away from how to get an exact, agreed definition of 'care,' or 'environmental benefit,' 'artistic/technological contribution' etc., and towards the willingness of agents to stake a particular definition. The risk of staking is the likelihood of certain defined events of 'care' etc. occurring.[95] This shift is critical, for

---

94 Something approximating this statement appears in Graham and David Dodd's 1934 book *Security Analysis*: the original text on investing according to a company's 'fundamentals.' The specific statement, however, is not in the book. It is often simply attributed to Graham, most notably by one of his students, Warren Buffett. See also Appendix 11.3 for elaboration.
95 The focus here is on outputs (for they are what is recorded in the ledger) although refer-

instead of claiming the capacity directly to value outputs-with-no-price we analytically 'sidestep' that problem, or approach it indirectly by valuing the performances that generate those outputs-with-no-price. Adopting a cost plus average return pricing model we can then determine an implied, approximate 'price' value for those outputs, but the critical goal is not to have a full set of output prices, but a full set of staking prices.

There is one more analytical link before that explanation is complete: why would someone stake a performance that produces outputs that have value but no market price and hence generates no revenue? The answer is clear, although we have to connect to issues addressed in Chapter 8 to explain it. It is that when the network attributes a token to that value creation, the token can be used to clear credit in the network. It means that creditors, and creditors of creditors, are recognising the creation of value. The capacity to clear credit becomes the ultimate network-wide recognition of value creation.

5.3 Returns to stakeholding

Agents will stake other agents' performances not merely to express views about what constitutes value, but in search of a yield. This includes a yield on outputs that are consumed in the commons.

The returns to staking will be in whatever form the staking contract nominates, but generally they are in two forms. First, there are changes in stake price. The full meaning of this awaits the introduction of tokens, and especially the credit token. It also awaits a consideration of the relation between internal and external financial units (e.g. fiat).

Second, stake will generate 'a dividend' (value-remuneration sharing). It may be a share of output, or a share of net revenue (outputs less the cost of inputs). It could be a financial return or a commodity output return, and those returns may accrue directly to the stakeholder or to some other agent nominated by the stakeholder, such as the commons (see Chapter 6). It could also give other rights; for example, rights to influence the future evolution of the performance, or it could give the stakeholder rights to build their own performance in connection with the performance they staked. Indeed, when outputs are framed as dividends, dividends themselves become the center of the governance and

---

ence is to outputs whose outcomes have been validated by the network..

innovation dynamism that drives the network. This depiction is central to the way 'surplus' is defined in the network.[96]

Notice, therefore, the investor intent that now becomes apparent in the act of staking when we focus on returns to staking. Agents stake a performance that they would 'like to see happen,' because it complies with their emotional and aesthetic perspective, because they believe the performance is important in the overall profile of the network, or because there is a distinctive dividend they would like to acquire, be it a physical package, access to something or simply an acknowledgment that the performance they staked generated a benefit for others. This reveals that ethical, emotional and aesthetic dimensions are embedded in the depiction of value, and the dividends on performances will therefore also embed those ethical foundations.

5.4 Staking and the network: a summary and a projection

Stake plays six critical roles in a network, some of which have just been described, others of which await the depiction of tokens, and especially the role of credit. We nominate the latter at this time, to give signals to readers who are looking to comprehend the network-as-a-whole, and especially its liquidity.

- *Resourcing performing.* Staking is a means by which agents enter the performance of another agent: staking opens 'relations of performing' which are not premised on wage labor or other extractive production relations.
- *Diversifying risk.* Staking enables the initiator/undertaker of performances to share the risks of their innovation, and mutual staking sees them diversify their own risks.
- *Collateral.* Stake stands as collateral for credit. The price of stake (reflecting future projections of its holders) therefore backs the credit that will fund other future performances.
- *Social Pooling.* Stake not only enables the diversification of risks (which is indeed one form of pooling); it also expresses the way in which individual agents who stake a performance combine to form a new agent defined by their common purpose (a new economic space), and in turn the way in which performances combine to form aggregated networks.

---

96 See Appendix 5.2 for elaboration.

- *Commensuration of performances.* Stake price makes all different performances commensurable, and hence creates the idea of an economy of collective innovation and interoperability among economic agents. But it does so, critically, without reducing the measurement of performances to a single index: it intentionally preserves the importance of diverse ways of measuring the value-creation of each performance.
- *Revealing network Value priorities.* When each performance is presented to the network in terms of the values it extols, staking choices are a voting process on values.

APPENDIX 5.1

FUNDAMENTAL VALUE AND SPECULATION: KEYNES' BEAUTY CONTEST

Keynes was critical of stock market speculation. He was writing in the context of the 1920s stock market boom and the 1929 crash which directly connected to the Great Depression of the 1930s. In his *General Theory of Employment, Interest and Money* (1936) he wrote of 'the euthanasia of the rentier,' referring not to a literal policy proposal but to the prediction that the lower interest rates he believed his policies would generate would mean that people could not live off the income stream of their assets. They would have to invest in 'productive' activities.

Keynes' critique of stock markets was that investors simply buy the stocks they think other people will buy, for the more people who want to buy a stock, the more its price will rise. Popular investing, he contended, has nothing to do with the underlying business proposition and assets of companies (often called the 'fundamentals') and everything to do with what investors think other people will do; indeed, what investors think other people think other people will do. It is apparent that, more than 90 years on, there is widespread adherence to Keynes' interpretation of the stock market, and especially its application to investors in volatile cryptoasset markets, where many tokens are made up of narratives that lack underlying assets ('fundamentals').

We have differentiated staking in the new economic space from stock market investing in a capitalist economy, albeit accepting certain parallels, and from other forms of staking in cryptoeconomics.[97] Nonetheless, does Keynes' caution about stock speculation apply to our proposals for reciprocal staking, especially in the light of a 2022 major downturn in crypto markets? We need to be clear about how our proposal is distinct from Keynes' dramatic critique.

---

97 See Chapter 1.4 for this differentiation.

Here is Keynes' critique. (Readers are asked to overlook the almost 100-year-old social presumptions of both the object being described and the language used to describe it.)

To identify the workings of investing in the stock market, Keynes used an analogy with a style of 1930s newspaper beauty contests in which readers were asked to choose the 6 prettiest faces from a page of 100 photographs. The prize, reported Keynes (1936: 156), was:

> awarded to the competitor whose choice most nearly corresponds to the average preferences of the competitors as a whole; so that each competitor has to pick, not those faces which he himself finds prettiest, but those which he thinks likeliest to catch the fancy of the other competitors.

It is important to note that the 'competitors' in Keynes' explanation are not the 100 faces in the 'contest', but the readers/voters. The terms of the competition, Keynes continued, generated a distinctive voting logic:

> It is not a case of choosing those [faces] that, to the best of one's judgment, are really the prettiest, nor even those that average opinion genuinely thinks the prettiest. We have reached the third degree where we devote our intelligences to anticipating what average opinion expects the average opinion to be. And there are some, I believe, who practise the fourth, fifth and higher degrees.

In application to the stock market, Keynes contended that investors were like the reader/voters, buying shares not based on any criteria of fundamental value, nor propositions about profit-making potential, but on investors' perception of what they think other investors will buy. So nothing matters but opinions, and opinions on opinions, or what they think other investors think others investors believe is the average opinion of the value of the asset. In other words, it's all a speculative bubble of popular opinion without substance and it's destined to burst.

Some readers may see a parallel between Keynes' beauty contest analogy and our depiction of the relation between staking and network determination of value. But that would be a misunderstanding.

The first thing to note is that Keynes's analogy in application to the stock market is itself limited. It mis-places the role of the central authority. It inserts a discrete 'prize', funded by a central authority, as the motive for playing, and the awarding of the prize ends the game. In the stock market, people may invest in response to popular opinion and may be 'ahead' or 'behind' on their balance sheets according to stock choice and timing. But over time the material basis of share prices will be revealed by what state-certified corporate accounts actually show to be the profit performances of companies. The state's role is not as a prize-giver to attract short-term audience participation but as a rule-maker to ensure reliable data.

Second, a direct analogy with our network proposal is flawed. In Keynes' beauty contest, the contestants are not the faces (as would be implied by the term 'beauty contest') but the newspaper readers/voters. With reciprocal staking, the analogy would be if the only people who can vote in the beauty contest are the 100 contestants; they can divide their votes into fractions, and there is no winner-takes-all 'prize': the prize is connectivity. So there is no 'winning' from voting for yourself and, directly or transitively, it is likely that everyone will be holding a partial vote for everyone else, so prizes are as much collective as individual.

If we think of the 100 people whose faces appear in the contest, each having their own ways of identifying facial attributes (their own measures of value), there will be built across the network not a speculative bubble but a system of facial recognition. Distributed determination of value is a system of network recognition of value.

Two years before Keynes' *General Theory* was published, the idea of fundamental value rose to new prominence with developments in the analytics of corporate accounts. Benjamin Graham and David Dodd published *Security Analysis* (1934), introducing the concept of 'value investing.' Their work has been made famous in the 21st century by Warren Buffett.[98]

The approach they took was to look at the intrinsic worth, or long-term 'fundamentals,' of a company and not be distracted by short-term share price volatility. The fundamentals include measures like company performance, profit margins, asset values, debt levels, etc.. The investment proposition was to use data on these fundamentals to reach an overall valuation of the company. This was then a guide to whether current stock prices were 'overpriced' or 'underpriced,' with direct implications as to whether the stock should be bought or sold at its current price.

Each of these fundamentals depicted by Graham and Dodd in 1934 is generally defined by reference to a distinctly capitalist economy and, we contend, an early to mid 20th century capitalist economy. In the 21st

---

98 Graham was Warren Buffett's teacher/mentor. Buffett has written an introduction to later editions of *Security Analysis*.

century, most of the largest and fastest growing companies in the world, when measured by market capitalization – such as Alphabet, Amazon, Apple, Microsoft and Tesla – have share prices far in excess of what Graham and Dodd's measures would recommend, and have done so for some time.[99] To label these prices as 'speculative' and 'bubbles,' especially when they have lasted so long, seems to be a misreading of underlying processes.

We believe that these stocks are symptoms of a change in what we should understand by 'intrinsic worth' and 'fundamentals.' Two factors are critical here. One is that the intangible assets that dominate these companies' balance sheets – software patents and brands – cannot easily be subject to Graham and Dodd's measures.[100] The second factor is that investors in these iconic 21st century companies are not simply speculators, nor are they simply 'factoring in' environmental, social and governance (ESG) qualifiers to their profit-driven calculus.[101] Many are taking an intentional long-term position on the future of the economy and wider society. In a changing world, they are investing in intentional modes of change. They are signaling financially what they believe in and what they project the future economic frontiers to be. Neither Keynes' depiction of speculation nor Graham and Dodd's depiction of intrinsic value appear able to capture this motivation.

For these reasons, we contend that stake and stake owners inside the network will not tend to behave the way Keynes described. But nor are the fundamentals the ones that Graham and Dodd described, for people's social, political and emotional responses to network potential are themselves part of the fundamentals. Accordingly, the Economic Space Protocol provides the data required to construct measures related to affect in the network, and hence to undertake a fundamentals analysis informed by the critical role of affect. But it will be up to agents to compile these data in ways that generate meaning as well as prediction.

---

99 Tesla did not turn a profit between 2002 and 2019 yet its capital value was greater than Toyota, despite the fact that it produced less than 5 percent of the number of vehicles produced by Toyota.

100 The proportion of these companies' assets classified as intangible is: Alphabet, 73 percent; Amazon, 81 percent; Apple, 96 percent; Microsoft, 93 percent; and Tesla 94 percent. See Brand Finance (2022).

101 Reference here is to the emergence of so-called ESG accounting to sit along profit and loss accounts. But as ESG accounts are scarcely quantified, they sit largely as ethical qualifiers to standard accounts; not as an alternative way of measuring.

APPENDIX 5.2

DIVIDENDS AND THE SURPLUS

'Surplus' is one of those terms in economics with many meanings, and it is not appropriate that we should aspire to give the definitive meaning here. Nonetheless, it is a term we are using, and so it needs some clarification in the context in which it arises analytically.

In the financial language that frames our approach, a surplus is a spread. In neoclassical economics, focussed as it is on exchange relations, the surplus is in individual relations between buyers and sellers: it is the spread between the price a buyer/seller would have been willing to accept and the price at which they do accept an offer. In Marx, surplus value is a class-based spread between the value of labor power (approximately equal to the wage) and the new value created by current labor. Piero Sraffa's (1960) adaptation of Marx, which has been an important underlying influence in our analysis, poses the surplus as the spread between the commodities used up in the process of production and the commodities created by the process of production. When we extend Sraffa from a commodity world to a financial world, the surplus is simply output values created that are not paid for. Non-payment is not about theft, but the capacity of human endeavor to create, such that inputs into production are not sufficient to account for the value of outputs.

The Sraffian depiction seems valuable because of its generality: the neo-classical depiction is simply about 'bargains' in trading – a depiction without useful social meaning – and Marx's is specific to capitalist relations between labor and capital. The Sraffian surplus includes Marx's surplus, albeit that the emphasis is not on extractive relations (i.e. that one class produces the surplus and another owns it) but its analytical benefit is that it can describe also a surplus in market-based, commodity producing societies that are precapitalist (late feudal) and a postcapitalist (a 'market socialist'[102]) economy. Sraffa's ledgers resonate with those

---

102 Sraffa was not particularly an advocate of 'market socialism': a term which arose in the

we describe in later chapters, and give us some tools to describe a post-capitalist surplus.

But Sraffa's depiction also has an immediate limitation for our purpose, for it is explicitly a depiction of a surplus created in a non-monetary, commodity-producing economy (recall Sraffa's major work is called *Production of Commodities by Means of Commodities*). If surplus is attributed to the human endeavor to create, then we should not presume that the creative outputs of that endeavor are only and always commodities produced for a market. We prefer the extended Sraffian conception of the surplus as 'outputs not paid for,' which gives us an open-ended framing of what constitutes an 'output.'

When our analysis opens up the conception of value in a postcapitalist economy we can also define the surplus as a spread. In the performance evaluation framework (see Appendix 4.1) the surplus is the spread between the value of network performance inputs and outputs, where outputs are valued by the network evaluation of the social outcomes they generate. In the derivative framing (Appendix 5.2) this spread is the value of the swap.

At this stage of the analysis we are now in a position to clarify (somewhat) the surplus of the new economic space. The surplus will take the form of dividends on stake, so it is appropriate to repeat the depiction of a dividend from Chapter 5.3:

> It may be a share of output, or a share of the net revenue (outputs less the cost of inputs). It could be a financial return or a commodity output return, and those returns may accrue directly to the stakeholder or to some other agent nominated by the stakeholder, such as the commons (see Chapter 6). It could also give other rights; for example, rights to influence the future evolution of the performance, or it could give the stakeholder rights to build their own performance in connection with the performance they staked.

That list is open-ended: it can be whatever an agent's performance specifies the intended dividend to be. Some part of these dividends are not surplus: they are the conditions of reproduction of the performances of stakeholders either directly (by being used as inputs in their per-

---

context of the 1920s Socialist Calculation Debate which Hayek claimed to have mastered (see Chapter 2.4). The proposition here is simply that he describes a surplus that could be framed in the context of 'market socialism.'

formances) or indirectly, by being sold to enable the purchase of other inputs. Indeed, in the case of the commons, where outputs may be allocated for free, the existence of dividends may be significant for the stake price of the producer, and *that* is essential to the reproduction of the producer's performance. We cannot, *ex ante*, specify what fraction is surplus and what is necessary for reproduction.

However, this is not the full surplus. The definition above is the aggregate of private surpluses. We must also recognize the possibility that the network overall is more than the sum of its parts: that the whole network is a performance, and hence a potential source of surplus. The formalization of this collective dimension must await the analysis of the total network. But it is important to emphasize the muti-dimensionality of that surplus, associated with the multi-dimensionality of network value.

Our framing of the network surplus, especially as the spread between the costs of performances and the outcomes of performances (including the new economic space performance) comes close to what Brian Massumi has called in his '99 *Theses*' 'processural surplus value' or the 'surplus-value of life.' Massumi's Thesis 16 states:

> Marx's definition of surplus-value hinges on the labor theory of value, according to which value is the quantity of labor-time that is 'congealed' in the product. Processual surplus value . . . is purely qualitative and concerns the intensity of lived potentials. It is surplus-value of life. Capitalist surplus-value and processual surplus-value are, of course, related, but they cannot be equated. The former is the systemic capture of the latter. Their difference—the difference between quality of activity as such and the derivation from it of a quantitative yield—is internalized by the system, to serve as its driving force. (2018: 16)

And elsewhere, by way of summary, the 'surplus value of life' is:

> an experienced value that is its own value, worth it for itself. This is a purely qualitative value. It is as incomparable as the timbre of a particularly pellucid note of music or the saturation of a breath-taking color. It is incommensurable, unexchangeable. It is such as it was, all and only that, and nothing more than how it was lived. It can be pursued on the smallest or most macro of scales, beginning from right where one is. No need to wait for the correct, final analysis (which will never come) before jumping in. No need

for the end-all up front (which will never happen). Any and every moment can yield surplus-value of life, provided the moment is intensely lived. (2018: 91)

The concept of surplus we are working with has some close parallel with what Massumi's idea of processural surplus value is reaching for, because value is determined by the processes of the network. But for Massumi, it is critical that the surplus-value of life is unquantifiable. Thesis 5 states that:

The first task of the revaluation of value is to uncouple value from quantification. Value must be recognized for what it is: irreducibly qualitative. (2018: 4)

Quantification, he believes, draws surplus back to the capitalist world of commodity production, at least until the concept of value can be reclaimed and freed from capitalist calculation.

Our analysis agrees with one aspect of this statement, which is why we contend that the surplus has no a priori categories of measurement. However, and here we are re-stating a proposition of our analysis made elsewhere (especially Chapters 5.4 and 11), if we focus on the social relationship of staking, and the propensity of agents to stake performances in the anticipation that those performances will create social-validated outcomes which the network can value via the identification of derivative spreads, then we are identifying the measurement of attributes of the surplus-value of life, even if that surplus is defined as beyond measurement.

CHAPTER 6

THE COMMONS

6.1 Finding the commons

In simple terms, a commons entails resources that have shared ownership and are built and curated in a distributed way. Particularly in a digital era, all sorts of performances and outputs are commons compatible. Non-divisibility of outputs and (close to) zero marginal costs of production, as found in software and other digital goods, are all conditions for a commons.[103] This suggests that commons attributes are everywhere: inside agents, between agents and across and between networks.

There is now an extensive literature on the ways in which p2p networks create the potential for a commons. We are strongly supportive of this broad agenda, and see a propensity towards participatory common ownership as integral to a postcapitalist vision.

We have already engaged issues that relate to the commons, but have not yet named them. One is reciprocal staking and the culture of risking together. Reciprocal staking is the mode of entry to the commons. The other is the exchange of particular commodities that have commons' properties. Some outputs will be 'public goods,' defined as outputs where one person's consumption does not preclude (indeed, may enhance) the consumption of others (for example data compiled by the network, public art, a clean environment). We believe that the second dimension is already well understood, and is not specific to the new economic space, so our focus is the commons that arises from mutual staking, or what we call the 'synthetic commons.' In finance the term 'synthetic' is used to describe instruments that are engineered to simulate the performance of other assets. In the Economic Space protocol, private ownership can, in certain circumstances, simulate the interests of collective ownership.

---

[103] The Creative Commons, for example, issues licenses to enable free distribution of an author's work for its further development. The license can limit the uses to which their work may be applied. See https://creativecommons.org.

Each of these is considered in turn.

6.2 Reciprocal staking forms the 'synthetic commons'

Although a commons is conventionally defined as the antithesis of private property, reciprocal staking creates the conditions for a commons via private ownership. If all agents in the network are reciprocally staked with all other agents either directly or transitively[104] then every agent is a partial owner of every other agent's performances. It may not be a large proportion of stake in the first instance, but it is significantly greater than zero. These are the conditions in which private ownership exhibits the same interests as common ownership: a synthetic commons. It is as if reciprocal staking across the network cancels out the effects (interests) of private ownership, for when each agent benefits from the success of every other agent, individual interests converge with collective interests.

It is not the intention of the new economic space that common interest be purely accidental. The proposal for enacting a synthetic commons is that each agent intentionally manages their reciprocal staking portfolio so as to secure a proportional reciprocal stake across the network. We term this combination of stake the 'commons asset profile.' Automated stake trading can find the optimal path for each agent (and all agents) to secure their desired holding of the commons asset profile. Some agents will seek a large holding of the commons asset profile; others less. The proportion of an agent's stake held in the commons asset profile determines the level of their access to the commons. So individual agents can choose whether to enter the commons and the level at which they hold membership. They can change this level by changing their reciprocal staking.

6.3 Dividends as the common purpose

Chapter 5.3 describes the dividends from stake ownership:

> It may be a share of output, or a share of the net revenue (outputs less the cost of inputs). It could be a financial return or a commodity output return, and those returns may accrue directly to the stakeholder or to some other agent nominated by the stakeholder, such

---

104 Direct staking is when two parties own a stake in each other. Transitive staking is where one party holds a staking exposure to another via a third party. If A holds stake in B and B holds stake in C, then A has a transitive staking exposure to C.

as the commons. It could also give other rights; for example, rights to influence the future evolution of the performance, or it could give the stakeholder rights to build their own performance in connection with the performance they staked. Indeed, when outputs are framed as dividends, dividends themselves become the center of the governance and innovation dynamism that drives the network.

An agent will enter the commons in order to acquire access to these dividends. Some performances for the commons will be of the same kind as performances not for the commons; it will be just the dividends that are available to the commons. Other performances will be commons-specific, in the sense that they are designed so as to be collectively accessible. For example:

- *Data.* The network will be 'spontaneously' producing a vast quantity of data that will be useful for each agent in order to monitor the health of the network and to inform their own decision-making. Yet each agent owns their own data, so that these aggregate data cannot be compiled and released without mutual agreement. The commons provides the means to co-ordinate and distribute network data. A condition of accessing collective data is that each agent must offer their own data in order to access collective data. Different levels of participation in the commons will be linked to different levels of data exchange and access.
- *Public goods.* There will be some outputs that benefit from scaled access. For some, there will be no exclusion. Agents in the network can access such outputs irrespective of whether they join the commons. But other performances have different attributes, where the possibility of scaling is large but exclusion is required (for example, a concert with a significant but limited audience capacity). These outputs may be offered to the commons. Access to these outputs (and their outcomes) could be conditional upon an agent's level of commons membership.
- *Free goods.* Some outputs are not produced so as to be sold, but they nonetheless produce value because they meet a recognized need within the network. We know they produce value because agents in the network are staking the performances that generate these outputs.[105] These outputs can be attributed a synthetic price (for purposes

---

105 The owners of stake in these performances receive yield in the form of appreciating stake price, but no *private* dividends. It could be that each individual investor is prepared to forgo yield because of a commitment to the commons. Or it could be that this com-

of data collection), and may be thought of as gifts to members of the commons (see Chapter 3.5).

In summary, the commons is brought into being by reciprocal staking and, once the conditions of a synthetic commons has been achieved, agents exchange dividends with the commons. There is no concept of equivalence in this exchange, for dividends are distributed directly, without the use of exchange offers. At a collective level these dividend offers to the commons constitute a social surplus: that part of network output which creates value that is not paid for.[106] The commons is a surplus distribution system! No agent has an incentive to hold back offers to the commons, and no agent's drawing down on the commons will restrict the capacity of other agents in the commons to draw down.[107]

6.4 The commons as a process of redistribution

The commons embeds some implicit processes of redistribution.

- *Assumed equivalence.* Because outputs for the commons are not priced, there is no formal calculation of what any agent puts into the commons and accesses from the commons: it is an assumed equivalence in a ledger sense. This assumed equivalence embeds a redistributional agenda: the *capacity* to contribute and the *need* to draw down.[108]
- *Underwriting lower-performing stake.* The requirement that agents will likely hold (directly or transitively) a proportional stake across the network gives temporary advantage to agents with lower-priced, lower performing stake, for all agents must hold some (small) exposure to

---

mitment is shared across the network, and demand for stake in these performances sees stake price escalate to 'compensate,' as it were, for the lack of private dividends.
106 'Not paid for' should not create the impression that it only applies to the outputs which would 'normally' be sold. Perhaps a better term is that applies to outputs that can be attributed only a synthetic price, as per Chapter 4.3.
107 Will any agent see a disincentive to hold stake in a performance which issues dividends to the commons, because they lose access to privately-accruing dividends? This would be a narrow reading of incentives, for to hold no stake in commons-linked performances would see this agent having limited access to the assets and products of the commons. So if the network as a whole judges a performance to be value-creating for the network, and its dividends are issued to the commons, each individual agent must hold some stake in that asset, directly or transitively, to access any part of the commons.
108 Reference here is to Marx's slogan from his 1875 *Critique of the Gotha Programme* (part 1): *'From each according to his ability, to each according to his needs.'*

these performances in order to hold the commons asset profile. Many of these performances will be in long-term decline, so the commons asset profile gives their stake some support to smooth the price trend. The threshold levels of reciprocal staking that constitute different levels of commons participation will need to be sensitive to this process.

The commons can also be designed as a system of intentional redistribution. The desirability, level and mechanisms of redistribution are matters of protocol design, so we here just nominate the sorts of mechanisms that might be implemented.

- *Absolute or relative reciprocal staking?* The process of agents' reciprocal staking as the mode of entry to the commons opens the issue of how to measure an agent's level of holding of the commons asset profile. Will it be the absolute level of mutual staking consistent with the commons asset profile, or the percentage of each agent's stake held in that portfolio? The latter clearly gives cheaper commons access to agents with smaller stake portfolios.
- *Decay to the commons.* Protocols could design the conditions under which the ownership of stake could revert to the commons directly or indirectly (i.e. to other agents in proportion to their commons membership). The condition of decay could relate to issues like activity on the network (dormant performances decay to the commons) or the size or concentration of ownership of performances (high priced stake or concentrated ownership could trigger conversion to commons ownership).[109]

These are all design principles for the *Commons Protocol* that await development, but it should be noted that any concerns about 'ultra-competitive' behavior in stake or commodity markets can be significantly ameliorated by the introduction of redistributional processes in relation to the commons.

---

[109] The possibility of decay to the commons, as a way to deal with the wealth effects of diverging stake prices, was raised in Chapter 5.2.

CHAPTER 7
POSTCAPITALIST UNITS OF MEASUREMENT

7.1 Introduction

The new economic space is an economic communication medium. Data generated from offers and their matches, netting and clearing provide agents in the network with access to a data pool for mining, interpreting and building new data performances. Some of these data performances will be for 'private' use within agents, others will be offered to the network; many of them through the Commons. They will be valued by the same process that all offers are valued. One of the most exciting potentials of the new economic space will be to see how data are assembled and spreads delineated, and how the network will feed off these analytics.

'How to measure?' is a critical proposition of postcapitalism,[110] for it will not be the same as in capitalism, where accounting practices 'lock in' calculative practices we have already contested.[111] There are multiple layers to this question, and two warrant attention. One is based on the distinction between capitalist and postcapitalist modes of measurement; a second is the distinctive measurement dimensions of distributed token issuance.

The measurement practices in capitalism take the form of an entrenched conventional wisdom. The units in which assets, liabilities and

---

[110] In the Socialist Calculation Debate, the principal area of disagreement between the advocates of central planning was what units should be recorded on ledgers: price or units of labor time or actual physical magnitudes of outputs and costs (called calculation *in-natura*).

[111] Analysis here would address the following sorts of practices: qualifying all exchanges as sales, so there can be no recording of outputs not for sale; seeking a positive delta between the sale price of inputs and the sale price of outputs, distributing this delta among shareholders, measuring an agent's credit worthiness and making valuations of investors dependent on this delta, and making the rate of return or interest the mode of commensuration and the calculative information that informs agent decision making.

outputs are measured and the units of exchange in relation to 'money' start with the presumed interconnection of capitalist accounting practices with fiat money. In that framing, measurement becomes reduced to price expressed in dollars. However, as we discussed in Chapter 2 in relation to Hayek, a focus on prices is important, but prices collapse social information to a single index, and strip market processes of much social meaning.

Nonetheless, the conventional wisdom is both deeply entrenched and embeds dubious assumptions. When it is explained, it generally takes the form of analogy about the benefits of a shared unit of measurement without asking how that shared unit came into being, and in whose interest it is sustained. The frequent analogy is with centimeters as a unit to measure distance and dollars to measure value. It's a false analogy. There is an international, invariant standard for a centimeter, preserved by the International Bureau for Weights and Measures; there is no such basis for a dollar and no one can explain precisely the purchasing power of a US dollar, or any fiat currency. Further, although a tape may be rolled out to measure distance, there is no such formula for asset value.[112] The hidden lesson from the analogy is telling: all measures are social conventions, but only some can be adopted as if they are invariant. Money and asset values are not in this subcategory and to assume that they are serves simply to displace their contestability into some other social dimension.

7.2 Measurement categories for the Economic Space Protocol

The Economic Space Protocol requires modes of measurement and financial encoding to quantify all sorts of changes at any given instant and over time. These will contribute to the network enacting new value forms in a way compatible with the network's ledger practices. Although not all are exclusive to a postcapitalist system, they will have distinctive postcapitalist dimensions to their compilation and use in explaining the behavior of the asset categories of stake, credit and commodities.

Below are the prevalent measures.

- *Measure of value.* The outcomes of performances must be measured in a way that network value cant be attributed. Every performance proposal

---

[112] A tape measure can verify that some spoons are 20 cm long and others 22 cm. No computation is needed. But to say one spoon is worth $2 and another $12 rests on social conventions of attributing value.

cannot be presumed to create 'value' for the network; the network must express an evaluation of whether the effects of the performance (its outcomes) are sufficient to be declared 'value.' The measurement here is related to the determination of 'what is sufficient' and it can only take the form of a spread between what was offered and what was then achieved. It cannot be a single network-wide unit of measurement (like a tape measure) for it is specific to each performance.

- *Market Offers.* These measure value in exchange. When matched, market offers are a way of measuring the rate of exchange at any given time between any two commodities, referred to as exchange value. When unmatched, exchange offers are understood to express views on potential exchange value. The exchange value of any asset can be calculated in terms of any other, but it is convention to use one specific asset to express these offers.[113] This asset is given the status of 'money of account' and is used to communicate exchange value in a standardized way. In the Economic Space Protocol, this asset is credit denominated in the unit of exchange.
- *Unit of exchange; unit of credit.* These measure commodity and credit rates of exchange. The unit of exchange is utilized as a common denominator in which to express exchanges, enabling the matching algorithm to gradually fill an order. Rather than 'deriving' the unit from the exchanges, we acknowledge its presence from the start, and express all exchange offers with it. This does not require credit, but just divisibility of the assets being exchanged in 'chunks' of these units. This unit becomes most visible to the users, when it is utilized to create units of credit which are, basically, credits measured in units of exchange.[114]
- *Commodity Specifications.* A distinct class of commodity (or particular attribute of multiple commodity types) can be compared qualitatively and quantitatively , A commodity specification is the aggregate of information (not just provided by the issuer of the commodities) that can be created by the network to enable a comparison.

---

113 In Chapter 1 of *Capital*, Marx referred to the relative equivalent forms of value, with the equivalent form as the benchmark against which other commodities are measured. Money becomes the 'universal equivalent.'

114 The unit of exchange and the unit of credit are similar, in the way a 100 dollar bill and a 100 dollar check are similar. Even though they both use the dollars as the measurement, they are two distinct instruments that pertain to two distinct accounts and two distinct risks. This distinction is clear from an accounting perspective, although not so much from a general use perspective.

- *Performance Metrics.* These measure the level of economic activity in the network. Associated with stake, a performance metric is derived from the records of the performance of an economic space, and compiled into distinct quantitative data that can be compared throughout time. As distinct forms of measurement and valuation, they are important benchmarks that influence the participation and the staking decisions of agents on a particular space. Anyone can create and publish a performance index, or adopt them. Performance metrics can be tokenized, be distributed as dividends, utilized as qualified and quantified forms of participation recognition, and/or exchanged in a market.
- *Offer matches over a unit of time.* These measure exchange value flow. We can trace the value flow between any two agents, or any two groups of agents by compiling the information contained in the offer records, where time can also be 'tick time,'[115] represented by the overall offer matching events, within the range being measured. This is valuable information for agents' credit issuance and staking decisions.
- *Stake exchange value.* This measures 'economic space agency.' It is important to measure the exchange rate of a particular space's stake in terms of units of exchange. The larger this value is, the larger the capacity of an agent to exert influence in the network, and express value. This unit compresses, but still retains, the assemblage of the qualities and quantities associated with an economic space.

The Economic Space Protocol challenges the traditional notion that exchanges must involve a money instrument in order to be executed. With distributed token issuance, tokens are not a store of value and stake is not converted to free-standing tokens when sold. Performance metrics, not just price, determine the network's valuation of an asset. Abstract units of exchange are deployed to increase the matching capacity of an exchange offer. These modes of measurement are associated with three distinctive exchange practices of the new economic space.

- *An abstract unit of exchange.* Exchange offers are expressed through an abstract unit of exchange, where the rates of exchange between any two commodities are translated to these units. Through netting, exchanges can occur without the need to hold and then use a mediating financial instrument (i.e. money). This is of particular importance,

---

115 On tick time, see Chapter 3.5.

since money in a capitalist economy is effectively the 'right to express exchange value.'
- *Reciprocally issued credit.* The Economic Space Protocol's money equivalent is reciprocally issued credit, denominated in units of exchange/units of credit. Agent credit issuance, like agent stake issuance, is determined by the lending/investing parties and is integral to the process of value determination in the network. Staking processes signal the network determination of value-creating performances; credit issuance and settlement through clearing – and the determination of what performance outputs can be credited – expresses value in a monetary form.
- *No interest credit.* Credit in the Economic Space Protocol does not generate interest payment in the capitalist sense. This frees agents from following the profit seeking heuristics of capital, and to focus instead on other forms of surplus transfer denominated in different units, and representing different measures of value (see Appendix 6.2). Dividends do not need to be converted into credits in order for them to be distributed. This is a different way of distributing the value that agents create, where an output (or an outcome), needs not be framed to be seeking a market.

7.3 Postcapitalist units of value

In Chapter 4.5 we introduced the term 'value theory of performance' which, in that context, was aspirational: why we would *want* to measure performances with respect to value. Yet how does a network actually attribute value when what constitutes 'value' is not predetermined?

This is a conspicuously different agenda from capitalist ways of measuring. In capitalist economies, the accounting conventions associated with 'value' attribution centers on the profit system, and those conventions evolved to express the calculative priorities of a profit-centered economy.[116] The price of a good or service is conditional on it meeting

---

116 The principle of standardized capitalist accounting first emerged in the 1850s, along with the legalization of joint stock companies (companies with shareholders) and limited liability. Investors needed standard performance metrics so that they could compare corporations and make informed investment choices and state protection against responsibility for the legal consequences of corporate actions. We know that these standard metrics, conventions and rules have been constantly evolving since then, but the connection of ledgers to profit has remained throughout. See, for example, Chiapello (2007),

profit conditions for its supplier (or supply will discontinue); the valuation of a capital asset is conditional on its expected future capacity to generate profit; the rate of interest and of rent charged are valued with the objective of securing a return for their providers at least equal to the rate of profit.[117] Optimisation models that sit on top of these categories are about valuing assets and determining their 'best' uses with respect to maximum profit. There are indeed debates about measurement, but they are within prescribed limits. They focus most prominently on issues like historical cost versus fair value accounting as the most appropriate way to record profit-centered measures.

When we open up the 'how to measure' question, the initial task, defined by the International Financial Reporting Standards (IFRS Foundation 2015:12), is 'recognition': 'the process of capturing an asset or liability for inclusion in the financial statements.' Capitalism has developed one system of recognition, but it is only a convention. In response, we can borrow from Keynes: 'the . . . conventional method of calculation will be compatible with a considerable measure of continuity and stability in our affairs, *so long as we can rely on the maintenance of the convention*' (1936:152, emphasis in the original).

The unit(s) of recognition of the new economic space are not bound by that convention. We can open up a range of different possibilities and build new, flexible conventions. The challenge is to reconcile flexible and multiple modes of recognition and measurement with the need for commensuration across the network.

We start with the conditions of flexibility, as they apply to each individual performance. The International Financial Reporting Standards (IFRS 'Conceptual Framework for Financial Reporting' (2018:A46-47)) identifies a ledger-expressed unit of account (not to be confused with the money

---

Levy (2014), Hopwood and Miller (1994) and Bryer (2000). Of course the proposition is not that everything in a capitalist society is expressed through profit criteria, but that this is the defining social feature of the era. Activities outside profit criteria are interpreted through the discourse of subsidies (and taxes), philanthropy or being classified simply as 'non-economic.'

117 Current conventional accounting can adopt a unit of 'capital' as its measure because capitalist accounting has been built for the specific purpose of defining and measuring 'capital.' This is the accounting dimension of the so-called 'Cambridge Critique' of capital theory which argues, in essence, that there is circularity in the conventional theory of capital: the value of capital cannot be specified until its rate of return is known and its rate of return cannot be known until capital is valued. See G.C (Harcourt 1972).

function of 'unit of account'). As defined there, a unit of account can be an asset-specific way of measuring and has the following features:

- It is selected for an asset or liability when considering how both recognition criteria (see Chapter 4.3) and measurement concepts will apply to that asset or liability.
- There may be multiple units of account, for example, one for recognition and another for measurement, and the components of the unit of account may change.
- It must faithfully represent the substance of the transaction or other event from which it has arisen.
- It must provide relevant information to the users of financial statements, and
- It is important to consider whether the benefits of the information provided to users of financial statements by selecting that unit of account are likely to justify the costs of providing and using that information.

The IFRS conditions give the mechanics to measure the distinctive outcomes of each performance's outputs, with careful attention to the differences between performance outputs and outcomes (see Appendix 4.1).

The offer of a performance (see Chapter 4.3 and 4.4) must include not just proposed outputs but also stated goals of social benefit (outcomes) of the performance, consistent with these IFRS conditions. Those outcomes could relate to the social effects of the outputs or of the performance process itself (its 'performing relations,' environmental footprint, etc.). The challenge is how those achievements are verified and validated by the network. This is less a technical exercise of calculation than a social process of evaluation.

In most conceivable claims to outcomes, an absolute measure may be impossible, for there is no baseline. So the objective, as with social impact bonds , is to create a measurable spread between two unmeasurables. In the social investment bond described in Appendix 4.1, the success of a policy intervention had no absolute units of measure, but the spread between a control group and an intervention group could be measured precisely.

How would this framing of a spread play out in the new economic space? It will be an iterative process of stake price spreads widening and narrowing. When a performance is offered for staking, the performing agent nominates some target outcomes that can be independently verified. Achieving these outcomes is the performer's claim to creating social value. It is the process of staking and the market for stake that will verify these claims to value creation.

Certain stakers may, after negotiation, make a positive financial evaluation of the potential for that performance to create outcomes which will meet the conditions of being declared 'value.' Those stakers have taken a risk, in anticipation of some form of reward. The rest of the network, which has not acquired stake in the performance, may nonetheless be evaluating the performance contract, perhaps changing their stake in the agents who have staked the performance. If the performance outcome targets are met, the outputs are declared to be value in the network (and validated for clearing credit in the network).

The rest of the network now declares its judgment. When outcome targets are met, the network may judge that those targets were in some way inappropriate. They express this by selling off their stake holdings in the agents who staked the performance. When the outcome targets of a performance are exceeded, the next circuit of performance will *probably* see higher outcome targets in the performance offer. This is a signal to the network that this performance is producing increasing amounts of value, and it will attract new stakers: its stake price will increase. Where targets are not met, the next circuit will *probably* need to set lower targets (or performance termination) and stake price will fall.

The underlying process is that the network's evaluation of the attribution of value to the outcomes of a performance plays out not attempting to attribute a direct price to those outcomes; it plays out as spreads on stake prices. Here we see an important reason not to collapse network information simply to stake price, for it can disguise the social meanings transmitted in the network, of which price is just one. 'Lying behind' the shifting staking prices are the simultaneous determination of what constitutes value and how claims to value creation are verified. Here, we see rich network data – economic media – as the bearer of the process of value expression.

7.4 Conclusion: basic categories

The proposition of the new economic space is that the condition of postcapitalist measurement centers on the mechanism by which agents in the network reveal their collective view of what constitutes value. The condition of measurement is that this expression be quantifiable in some way.

The processes of the Economic Space Protocol provide the mechanism for the determination of a range of measures by which to monitor and evaluate. Some are generated across all performances and become indices of comparison on the basis of which analytical propositions can be built. Others are constituted as spreads, designed to capture the subjective evaluations of agents. They can all be critical measures, but because they are calculated differently, they are not reducible to a single measure.

Value measures, for example, cannot be directly expressed in prices for they are not expressions of exchange although, we conjecture, they will be indirectly expressed through stake price movements. We anticipate the network will create many indices of activity and measures of performance: they will themselves be a field of performances.

CHAPTER 8

LIQUIDITY AND CREDIT

8.1 Introduction

An implicit assumption to date has been that markets are liquid. It is a widespread assumption in economics and has enabled all sorts of theories to simply ignore or marginalize the question of illiquidity, especially at the level of individual agent relations. It is a misleading assumption. Agents face what Perry Mehrling (2011), following Hyman Minsky, calls 'the survival constraint.' Expressed simply, '[i]f you can't roll your funding as it comes due, you are dead.' This constraint goes to the heart of exchange, and we see it manifesting everywhere as businesses going broke and people losing their homes due to illiquidity.[118] Yet for Hayek, market participants agree to a price but there is no bid-ask spread;[119] for Marx, commodities are assumed to exchange at their value, and illiquidity is framed as a source of crisis, not as an integral variable of exchange. Indeed, in Chapter 3, where we first introduced our categories of exchange, we explicitly assumed market liquidity for the simple reason that liquidity is a system-wide issue: it can only be understood in the context of the flows of the overall network, and that's not the place to start an analysis.[120]

We know liquidity to be contingent on the social relations that secure ongoing capacity in market processes, and those social relations are themselves unstable. An economy based on staking performances is always opening a time interval between the performance offer and recovery of costs of mounting a performance, or the time taken for the

---

[118] It should also be noted in this context the trillions of dollars (or other fiat currency) of central bank 'quantitative easing,' for the explicit purpose of propping up liquidity in financial asset markets.

[119] This point is central to Sraffa's critique of Hayek: that when supply and demand are not in equilibrium, there is a difference between the spot rate and the forward rate. This spread forms the concept of commodities having an 'own rate of interest' (Sraffa, 1932: 50). This framing fed into Chapter 17 of Keynes' *General Theory* (1936).

[120] Marx would make the same claim.

completion of a 'circuit of performance' (to use a term adopted in Chapter 11.2).[121] Volatility and liquidity are tied together. These issues can now be addressed, although further layers of understanding will also be added in later chapters.

The key to liquidity is access to credit. Credit is an IOU. In the Economic Space Protocol, credit gives an agent the right to amend the network ledger – to match an offer and issue a token – when that token is, in effect, provided by another agent. But to frame credit as just a personal relationship between two agents would miss its significance in the network, for the issuance of these IOUs also connects directly to issues of securing network liquidity. In the absence of centrally-issued money, and the associated capacities of a central bank to regulate liquidity, distributed issuance of credit performs money-like functions that must create and sustain liquidity. In this chapter we address the issuance of IOUs and the conditions of their settlement (credit clearing).

A second role of credit for liquidity is the network's requirement of credit to enable exchanges that can not be performed without granting a delay in their payment. We will consider this second role in Chapter 9.3.

It is important to address at the outset of a consideration of credit a widespread popular perception that debt (the flip-side of credit) involves the social and financial subordination of borrowers to lenders. It is a relationship predicated on extraction. We share that view. Our focus on credit rather than debt is not semantic. Credit is about connecting the present to the future and no economy can work without credit. It secures network liquidity and brings forward the capacities of agents to create that future. Debt re-expresses credit by reference to the attached obligations; invariably with a focus on interest payments. But in the new economic space there is no role for interest payments and no incentive for any agent to agree to pay interest on credit. One of the expressions of distributed issuance of credit is that it brings to the attention of every agent the contingency of liquidity and their own capacity to alleviate illiquidity. It is in their own interest to issue credit; it doesn't need the payment of interest.

8.2 The general conditions of distributed credit issuance

Two agents may contract a credit relationship on any terms they choose but, for wider applications, there needs to be network recognition of

---

[121] Reference here is to Marx's circuits of capital in Volume II of *Capital* (1885, Part 1) and our own interpretation of a performance circuit in Chapter 11.1 and 11.2.

credit that is not based on direct personal relations.[122] Our analysis has already established the proposition that credit in the new economic space must meet the following conditions:

- It has distributed issuance.
- It uses distributed staking as collateral.
- It is recognized and validated across the network.

The analytical challenge is that a distributed process must express some form of collective cohesion. The Economic Space Protocol must create the conditions for that cohesion.

One dimension of cohesion is that the network needs a unit in which credit will be issued and repaid: a general unit of credit. In Chapter 6.2 it was determined that the general term is 'unit of exchange,' but when extended to intertemporal exchange it will be referred to simply as a 'unit of credit.' It is the conditions of repayment where the analytical challenge lies, for those conditions must be created within the network and reflect its calculative processes.

So our analysis must restate the three conditions; particularly the second and third.

Distributed issuance

As an agent-to-agent relationship (more precisely, an agent-to-network-to-agent relationship), distributed issuance has come up in earlier chapters. In itself, it is a straightforward process. All agents have the capacity to offer and/or accept credit to/from other agents. This means that each agent is not just a producer, participating in performances, and an investor, staking other agents' performances, but also a 'bank,' issuing and receiving credit.[123]

We understand that some readers will immediately be skeptical about the idea of agents being banks, for they will see banks as being at the core of the problem of capitalism; not a means of its transformation. The idea that all agents can be banks is rhetorical when we think of banks as institutions, but the idea that all agents can be issuers as well as receivers and

---

122 See the condition of recognition, described in relation to outputs, but applying in the same way to credit, in Chapter 4.3.

123 Although this phrase could describe a Local Exchange Trading Systems (LETS), where the term 'mutual credit' is used to describe the creation of IOUs, we are referring to scalable, tokenized credit.

clearers of credit is entirely serious. Indeed this is at the center of Hyman Minsky's approach to finance:

> To analyze how financial commitments affect the economy it is necessary to look at economic units in terms of their cash flows. The cashflow approach looks at all units – be they households, corporations, state and municipal governments, or even national governments – as if they were banks. (1986: 221)

In a protocol framework, the proposition is that the recording on a ledger of each individual agent's borrowing and lending is the same whether this agent is a person, a household or an assembly of people. We therefore turn to the capacity of agents and the network to 'be banks' and issue (and clear) credit, and the critical dimension here is staking.

8.3 Stake as collateral: the foundation of credit

The capacity to issue credit has already been prefigured as a network logic, but without being named as credit. The model of stake issuance introduced in Chapter 5.2 is implicitly a credit-issuance logic.

A basic credit-issuance logic, standard in financial economics, is that a bank issues dollar credit of its own *private* creation. The dollars it issues are used by the borrower to make payments to others, who deposit their received money in their own bank, which may be different from the borrower's bank. The private issuance is now accepted by the depositor's bank; indeed that bank will not know the direct source of the money it has taken on deposit. There has simply been the acceptance/absorption of the newly created money: it has been declared to be money. The privately-issued money is now part of the banking *system* and thereby validated as *social* money.[124]

Similarly in relation to stake in the Economic Space Protocol. An agent in the new economic space creates stake by *privately* investing in other agents and receiving investment from other agents. These investments now appear to the *network* as an agent holding a portfolio of stake, which is taken *socially* as collateral for credit. The issuance of stake involves stake ownership rights being declared as an asset. It is essentially the same logic as banking. By analogy, when each agent in the network not

---

[124] This isn't the skeptic's view of banks and money creation, it is the view of the Bank of England. See McLeay, et al (2014) and Bank of England (2014).

only undertakes performances but acquires stake in other agents' performances, and uses that stake as collateral for credit issuance, each agent is a producer, an investor and also a bank.

Once the network can bring a portfolio of stake into existence, analytically it is straightforward to count that stake as collateral, declared in the network's unit of exchange. Stake then becomes collateral for a line of credit issued in that same unit of exchange, now simply renamed a unit of credit.

Several propositions follow from this simple connection:

- *All credit can be fully collateralized.* Lenders can nominate their required level of collateral, so individual agents will be operating with banking capacities akin to those of shadow banks.[125] This adds stability to the lending (minimizing default risk), and the costs of any default will be borne across the network.
- *Credit has a material basis.* The claims attached to stake ownership give a material basis to credit.
- *Expanding stake expands credit.* There is an ongoing incentive for agents who are developing a performance to issue stake on that performance, and to buy stake in others, for the more stake they acquire, the greater their capacity to secure credit.

The proposition embedded here is that the value of stake-as-collateral can be priced and verified across the network. Each agent is therefore aware that the path to their own liquidity is to issue liquidity to others. This is not merely an ethical exercise of mutual support, though it will embrace that. The point is that, in the design of the Economic Space Protocol, there are no disincentives to any agent issuing collateralized credit when the network faces illiquidity, and hence no grounds for interest payments.

8.4 Network recognition of credit and credit settlement

When the network adopts a capacity for credit issuance, credit itself becomes the liquid expression of the unit of exchange and the key to the verification of value within the network. Credit is the means to express all value in the network in the same units. The process here is critical to understanding the new economic space and the proposition that a

---

125 Note the definition of shadow banking in footnote 24.

network that has no central issuance of money (no conventional 'money') can nonetheless have network-wide credit at its core.

A simple proposition is the key. All stake is different, but all credit is of the same kind. We first explain the proposition before clarifying how it is key.

Each unit of stake is a holding in a different performance, undertaken by a different agent. The differences between each stake are important, for acquiring a range of stakes gives an agent the diversity of risk exposures in their stake portfolio. In aggregate, the linked diversity of reciprocal staking gives the network a common investment in a network future: there is unification via risk sharing ('risking together').

But credit is all of the same kind, and its fungibility is integral to its role. It is denominated in the network's unit of exchange (hence the unit of exchange is also the unit of credit) and it can be used throughout the network: credit is not tied to the particular performances that formed the collateral of credit. In simple terms, the IOUs of credit can be used for transactions across the network and can be repaid across the network. Put slightly differently, within a network of credit, where agents are both borrowers and lenders, no agent can know which particular chain of credit they link to,[126] so there is a logical demand for a common unit in which to express credit (Doepke and Schneider 2013).

It follows that liquidity arises not through exchange ('monetized barter') but through commensuration across a network, and its form of expression is in credit.

What, then, is the significance of the identification that all stake is different and credit is universal? Here we have to 'loop back' and recall that staking is the way in which agents in the network express their relative views on what performances contribute to network value (Chapter 5.2). The incentive in staking is to invest in the performances that you believe make the greatest contribution of aggregate, network value. The outcome of the aggregate of these staking decisions is the collective determination of that network value. The dialectical relationship between the choice of staking and the value of stake is integral.

At the point of the analysis where this valuation process was initially described, it could only be expressed in relative terms, as staking ratios. But credit and liquidity open the path for these ratios to be expressed

---

[126] Fleischman et al.(2020) offers an interesting twist on this proposition: the identification of credit loops which could be cleared by the temporary injection of an agreed monetary unit.

in the unit of exchange; as prices, and given the appearance of absolute measures.[127]

The simplest way to see this is in the question of what pays down credit, or how an agent works off an IOU. An agent who uses credit to create and offer a performance to the network is, in 'normal' circumstances, creating outputs that get verified by the network as the creation of value via the attribution of a price, in processes already explored (Chapter 4.2). This created value can be used to clear credit, no differently from the way income is used to repay a bank loan.

Here is the critical development. So long as the network has endorsed an output as value (and given a price in one of the four ways described in Chapter 3.5), the agent who granted the credit is not concerned about what particular outputs are produced to repay their credit, for it shows on their ledger simply in the network's unit of exchange/unit of credit. Nonetheless, 'behind the scenes,' clearing credit will often involve not just two but multiple agents across the network. Even though credit establishes a value exchange flow, by linking two agents, value exchange will flow across multiple links.

This is the same process by which output produced for the commons can be attributed value on the network ledger: when it is executed through a credit process, the (network-endorsed) value which is given away can nonetheless appear on a ledger as a positive value when it is part of clearing credit, for it is automatically converted to the network unit of exchange.

8.5 Implications

While a single exchange may be the simplest of economic acts, generalized monetary exchange requires the most developed of foundations. Exchange needs an intertemporal dimension: it requires *future exchange credits*, expressed in the unit of exchange. For shorthand, we call it the *unit of credit*.

The articulation of credit in relation to stake now appears at the core of the Economic Space Protocol logic. It has been said multiple times that the network faces a challenge of binding the present to the future in the absence of an active central authority (state). We now see that credit and stake form an intertemporal double helix. Stake binds the network by generating unity out of diversity (portfolio theory); credit binds the

---

127 It is only an appearance, and should always be acknowledged as such.

network by giving value coherence to diverse performance outputs (unit of exchange, expressing a theory of value).[128]

As our analysis moves from performances to staking to credit, we move closer to the centrality of ledgers recording all transactions as assets and liabilities denominated in a common unit of exchange. This points directly to the domain of tokens.

---

128 Reference here is to a value theory of performance (Chapter 4.5).

APPENDIX 8.1

KEYNES ON MONEY AND CREDIT

Most economic theories built 'from the ground up' start with exchange. Hayek's theory is pure exchange, where money is just the assumed medium. Marx began *Capital* with simple exchange – linen for coats – so as to 'discover' that they have abstract labor in common as their point of comparison (and equivalence). The populist history of economics starts with an allegory that once there was barter and then the limitation of the 'double coincidence of wants' led to the 'invention' of money as a means of exchange. This depiction is misleading for in many contexts credit/debt is the precondition of trade, but analytically it suggests that economic relations start with specific/unique outputs and only later 'invent' or logically derive the generality of money.[129]

Money does not come into being as a means of exchange but as credit. That embeds money deeply in social relations, for while trade occurs in a moment of time, credit is a relationship over time, and those relations cannot be assumed stable, either in themselves or in their economic context.

Of all the leading economic thinkers of the past, it is most conspicuously Keynes (and later Minsky) who gives focus to the conditions of money. Keynes supposedly 'solves' the problem of money and volatility via state policy, where a state monetary authority is the *deus ex machina* of the 'laissez faire' economy, providing the economy with a money instrument, secure banking for credit issuance, and the stabilization capacities of a central bank. For obvious reasons, it is not a 'solution' we care to adopt; in part because it turned out to be no solution at all.

Nonetheless, the fact that Keynes was analyzing the nature of money at a critical turning point in its history – the end of the 19th century gold standard – resonates with the current period. His proposal in the 1930s was that the state must 'back' money; called 'chartalist money.'[130]

---

[129] The standard source of this critique is Graeber (2011).
[130] His view was that while money could logically be denominated in any unit that has its

A century on, with the capacities of cryptotokens, that necessity for the state is being challenged. But the core questions Keynes posed are broadly consistent with what we face in contemporary cryptoeconomics.

In his 1930 *Treatise on Money*, Keynes contended that clearance comes not simply via price agreement between buyers and sellers, but via credit.

> Money comes into existence along with Debts, which are contracts for deferred payment, and Price-Lists, which are offers of contracts for sale or purchase. (1930: 3)

With distributed and mutual token issuance, a token, denominated in the unit of exchange, does not exist prior to the offer (i.e. the opening of a process of exchange). An offer of a token in return for a commodity (be it a good, service or another financial asset) is itself the creation of money: first as available credit (the offer) which is matched (the mediation or 'medium' in the exchange) and validated and settled through the verifiable exchange of commodity-backed tokens.

Keynes gave significance to this time interval in a way that Hayek could not. His focus was to account for the way agents deal with uncertainty, and the way the state manages potential illiquidity (and crisis) implied by uncertainty. This is of central importance also in a distributed cryptoeconomy, and we can follow Keynes' approach. In 1933 he wrote an important essay called A *Monetary Theory of Production*:

> The distinction which is normally made between a barter economy and a monetary economy depends upon the employment of money as a convenient means of effecting exchanges – as an instrument of great convenience, but transitory and neutral in its effect. . . That, however, is not the distinction which I have in mind when I say that we lack a monetary theory of production. An economy, which uses money but uses it merely as a neutral link between transactions in real things and real assets and does not allow it to enter into motives or decisions, might be called – for want of a better name – a real exchange economy. . . . The theory which I desiderate would deal, in contradistinction to this, with an economy in which money plays a part of its own and affects motives and decisions and is,

---

own rate of interest (for example corn or coal, where the rate of interest is the change in its own price), the state's money is superior for it is generally accepted. See Keynes 1936: Ch.17.

in short, one of the operative factors in the situation, so that the course of events cannot be predicted, either in the long period or in the short, without a knowledge of the behaviour of money between the first state and the last. And it is this which we ought to mean when we speak of a monetary economy. (1933, pp.408-9)

In all forms of money, including cryptomoney, the process of offer matching is the source of spontaneous liquidity. In contrast with chartalist money, all agents can participate within the same exchange network, and offer matching is mediated through a common asset type (or unit of exchange). Netting enables exchange and settlement to occur without the need to actually hold the common asset. This monetary system can secure liquidity without the need for central control of issuance/un-issuance of a money instrument. A distributed exchange protocol[131] therefore constitutes the backbone of a distributed clearing house and a payments and settlement system.

---

131 See López, J. 'Market offers: Distributed trading protocol.' http://marketoffers.manifold.one

CHAPTER 9

EXCHANGE RELATIONS EXPRESSED THROUGH TOKENS

9.1 Context

The previous chapter commenced with a statement about why, contrary to the economics textbook order of exposition, it is appropriate to explain the 'full' process of exchange only after an explanation of credit, for processes of exchange require the presumption of an already-existing network with a unit of exchange and that network requires credit for liquidity.[132]

Conventionally-conceived markets specify the rights of buyers and sellers as they come together in a 'market place.' The analytical point is the individual who comes to market. The Economic Space Protocol recognizes these rights and adds additional foundational layers of rights compared with those attributed to a 'citizen.'[133] However, when analysis starts with a single agent, interactions across agents in a network can often go unacknowledged. Our focus on economic space gives that acknowledgement: the context is not a 'market*place*,' but a 'market*space*' or exchange network. These shared (distributed network) protocols frame the formalized rights and the responsibilities of agents and become the foundations upon which contractual relations can be created.

These relations all have expression in protocol accounting operations. There will need to be many such operations and hence many network conventions built. Our objective is not an exhaustive coverage of these requirements, but to reference illustrations of the style of these protocol requirements and show how protocol design transitions from conceptual proposals about the nature of markets, tokens and prices to formal

---

132 Here we are in parallel with Marx (1939: 259), explaining the development of the concept of capital:
 . . . it is necessary to begin not with labor but with value, and, precisely, with exchange value as an already developed movement of circulation.

133 But note the caution expressed in chapter 2.2.

ledger-based practices. The issues we have chosen to illustrate are those that were core to our initial reframing of markets in Chapter 3: the processes of offer issuance, matching, netting and clearing. This and the following chapter are expositions of those processes.

9.2 Reciprocal Issuance: offers and matching

Exchange between any two (or more) parties can be framed as an exchange of rights and expressed on a balance sheet as a transfer of assets and liabilities. This framing is what Perry Mehrling calls 'the money view' of exchange, for it records, as a bank does, assets and liabilities rather than income and expenditure accounts.[134] So the recording of a simple good or service sale sees the seller gain an asset in the form of a token and the loss of an asset (a commodity) of equal value. The buyer has a reciprocal movement – the acquisition of the commodity and the liability of a payment of a token. The formal expression of Mehrling's money view is consistent with the requirements of protocol design.

An offer is a statement of the rights an agent is willing to give and the rights they are seeking to receive from *any* other agent in the network. Reciprocal issuance is the realization of an offer as a formal agreement between two or more *specific* agents. This would make no sense prior to the development of distributed network applications, for there would be no credible basis for trust in distributed issuance. But a network ledger and exchange protocol provides a basis for verification: protocols, in a contractual form of rights on one side and duty or obligation on the other, can enable agents to have confidence that making offers and their matching, recorded on a ledger, will replace the role currently performed by the state's money and central and private banks.

When an exchange occurs in a network, whether it be for commodities or stake, we depict traders as making offers to either exchange commodities/stake for credits (buy), or credit for commodities/stake (sell). But this is not the conventional simple exchange of the economic textbook, and in two critical ways:

---

[134] This and the following chapter – indeed the whole framing of token markets – draws on the 'money view' of economic analysis of Perry Mehrling (n.d.). For a summary see Saeidinezhad (2020).

- *The whole network is involved.* Exchange is not between two autonomous agents, but between each agent and the network. This is more than a statement that the seller may not know or meet the buyer. It is that the process of offer-matching, netting and clearing requires the whole network of participants (and its full set of protocols) on the other side of the contract.[135] The need for this complexity is integral to scalability and liquidity[136] of the network and it differentiates the Economic Space Protocol from many p2p systems that require direct matching or personal relations to secure trust in the process.
- *The time interval of exchange is critical.* In the conventional economy, money 'solves' the time interval because it stands in for the other commodity: a commodity can be exchanged for money and money later converted to another commodity. In the equivalent process in the Economic Space Protocol, an offer must be matched with an acceptance by another agent. There may be a direct match on offer but, if not, the network must find a coordinated set of matches, and matching may require a temporary issuance of network credit to 'buy time' in order to generate a match.

Tokens are transferable and quantifiable bundles of rights, whose ownership gets recorded through a ledger. Tokens themselves hold no mystery: they are simply a representational device that point to 'real' assets. As these transfers are specific, so the tokens that represent them are specific,[137] and as the transfers are between two agents, mediated by the network, so tokens can only be issued by agents (not centrally). It follows that tokens have a corresponding right – a commodity, stake or credit – that they represent. They are, in essence, (smart) contracts which trigger ledger entries.

The key to token ledgers is that the token and the 'real' item move in opposite directions. For example, an agent who offers a good or service to the network will receive a token specific to that offer in acknowledgment of the offer being matched. More specifically, the act of matching offers validates the offered outputs (be it good or service, stake or credit),

---

135 See López, J. 'Market offers: Distributed trading protocol.' http://marketoffers.manifold.one

136 Liquidity comes with the capacity of the matching algorithm to increase matching opportunities.

137 The liquidity token is different, for it is defined precisely by its universal expression.

resulting in the issuance of a token from the accepting agent to the offering agent. Note that it is not a promise to deliver an output to a buyer; it is a confirmation by the traders that the exchange of rights have been successfully completed.

In summary, in a network context:

- Ledgers record assets and liabilities, not income and expenditure *per se*. The focus is on changes in stock and the flows that generate those changes.
- Credit, we saw in Chapter 8, is the key to network liquidity. The network presumes that agents hold lines of credit, for it is through credit that token transfers settle.
- For any agent the object of clearing credit is not to be free of credit, for that would mean free of liquidity, but to open the space for new credit offers. Paying down a line of credit is the equivalent of a payment because it enables an agent to acquire more credit equal to the paydown.
- The network discovers the importance of a shared unit of exchange to commensurate credit between different agents. The unit of credit arises from the unit of exchange, as credit's fungibility makes it the most liquid form of exchange. Functionally, a unit of credit emerges not only to enable relations of exchange, but to enable credit changes that result from exchanges to be cleared.

9.3 Netting and clearing

In the Economic Space Protocol both netting and clearing are a network process, where every agent participates and collectively assumes the role commonly taken by a specialized third party like a clearing house. This is a distributed exchange protocol, and it enables four levels of exchange:

- *Exact match.* This is where token offers can match one to one. The ask of an offer is the bid of another, and vice versa. It is tokenized barter.
- *Partial match.* This is where the token offers are partially matched, and require several commodity matches to fulfill the offer. This is fractional tokenized barter.
- *Mediated match.* This is when two offers are matched through a third asset, but that asset itself is netted away. In this process, the unit

of exchange performs the role of measuring the asset in a way that makes it universally recognized in the network.
- *Credit mediated match.* This is when two offers are matched, through time, and mediated through a credit-giving instrument. In the following chapter, we identify this instrument as the liquidity token.

Exchange mediated through a unit of exchange and recorded on a ledger involves a process of netting: the simultaneous exchange of each party's asks and bids. More complex exchanges, lacking the 'double coincidence of wants,' require more complex ledger processes, involving an interval of time and a token (credit) that can stand for a commodity offer that awaits matching. Here, netting of the ledger is a clearance process.

In conventional markets, this is the function of (central) clearing houses that rely on records of flows inward and outward from multiple clients in order to net and clear the market. Where there is an exchange to money before conversion to another commodity, credit is being offered to the seller, and there is a clearing function.

In the Economic Space Protocol, when an agent has different offers but where the unit of exchange is present simultaneously in the ask and the bid component, offers may be netted, using the unit of exchange as means of computing their exchange rate. Hence, the common asset itself does not need to be 'owned' nor exchanged.

As the network scales, there is diminishing likelihood of direct matches in the barter process: 'blockages' become more pervasive and netting starts to require an interval of time for the 'discovery' of a netting pathway.

To find matches for offers on the network, the protocols of the network will 'induce' moments of credit to remove 'blockages' (illiquidity) in the netting and clearing process. This is an additional role of credit in the network to that identified in the previous chapter. The time interval implicitly requires the creation of credit, which can be retracted when the match is found. It is the oil that lubricates the netting process: it temporarily 'stands in' for different sorts of commodities (or stakes) in the facilitation of the netting process. As the network scales, and the 'blockages' in direct netting become more pervasive, the role of liquidity via credit grows. In the process, the unit of exchange/credit consolidates its role as the universal unit of commensuration.

9.4 Economies enabled by protocols

The processes defined in this chapter are, in effect, the application of concepts developed in Chapter 3. There, key concepts were being differentiated from conventional framings of markets, prices and money. They perhaps appeared simply as asserted redefinitions. By now we can see what those redefinitions have enabled: the broad dynamics of the network-as-process that can be expressed on a ledger. This is an insight into the sorts of dynamics the Economic Space Protocol must design and enable and the ledger-expressed procedure that design expresses. The resulting 'network awareness' enables us to reason about the economy – its agents and its artifacts – as protocols. Awareness also means that protocols will be created so as to be redesignable by the network. This ensures that protocol design will remain current and fit for purpose.

The following chapter takes this identification further, to look at the exchange of commodities) stake and credit as ledger-based, and hence token centered, processes.

APPENDIX 9.1

TOKENS AND NETWORK DERIVATIVES

In conventional markets, derivatives are understood as tools of risk management, delineated as futures, options and swaps. They involve ownership of attributes of an underlying asset, but no necessary ownership of that asset itself. Those attributes are generally related to price spreads, but could in principle apply to any index constructed to describe the underlier.[138]

To frame reciprocally-issued tokens as derivatives opens up three related issues.

- *Exposure to the future.* They are both statements about the future, and the formation of possibilities. Token issuance is about their potential to be validated (backed) by a network, so they embody an exposure to the future of that network.
- *Quantified social relations.* In an economy based in issuance, redemption and settlement, the token immediately implies a quantified social relation. Tokens represent what we call 'network derivatives.' This depiction signals that token types give a partial 'exposure' to the total social relations: we are 'decomposing the social' via different token categories, in a way that cannot be done by a singular, centrally issued coin.
- *Attributes of assets.* Derivatives imply classification or bundling. Each oil option contract, for example, is distinctive in its detail (they have different prices because they are written on different prices of oil,

---

138 Weather derivatives, for example, trade spreads on indices of frost, temperature, etc.. Sports betting involves trading spreads on all sorts of game metrics, not just the final outcome. These are illustrations of non-price indices constructed to describe an underlier of which there is no owner. What is interesting here is that quantification counts 'events': the number of times X happens over a period, whether X is a frost or a tackle in a football game. Quantifying things by how often they occur – 'events' – is at the core of the way we define performances (see Chapter 5.3). If we use the occurrence of events to measure time, we are in the domain of what financial markets call 'tick time' (see Chapter 3.5).

have different expiry dates and different strike prices). But they have a recognized common (formulaic) relation to oil such that they are priced relative to each other, giving future oil a set of continuous prices. Similarly, each individually-issued token must be recognisably a 'member' of a type, so each token within a network must be recognisable as a version of the tokens issued by others.

In summary, tokens are mutually recognized exposures to the output value that defines the network. This is the sense in which they are derivatives. Each token's strike price is determined by the network's expression of the value of a bundle of output values which is deemed to back a token.

CHAPTER 10

TOKENS AND LEDGERS

10.1 Introduction

Our analysis is now in the domain of ledgers and tokens. We need to present the relations of exchange, credit and staking as formal, ledger-expressed processes in contrast with earlier chapters, where those relations were depicted as social interactions. Connections between socio-historical and formal ledger modes of expression should be highlighted. They are not an easy fit but for protocol design they must be reconciled because it is vital to have both dimensions expressed.

Ledger representations give precision and transparency to social relations and social relations give the token and ledger representation a direct connection to material social and economic underliers. This two-way expression is our claim that the Economic Space Protocol is the depiction of 'real' economic processes: it is based socially in claims to historical change and economically in claims to a foundation in 'fundamental value.'[139]

Our focus in this chapter is the mechanics of exchange representation on ledgers. Following the order of exposition we have developed in previous chapters - starting with staking and moving to liquidity and then to dynamic (as opposed to simple) commodity exchange, we introduce the stake token, the liquidity token and the commodity token.

- *Stake tokens.* These will be issued by an agent in return for a stake in another agent's performance. It gives the holder the right to participate in the revenue (receive a dividend) and is generated by the issuing agent's economic activity.[140]
- *Liquidity tokens.* These are an extension of credit denominated in the unit of exchange, giving rise to units of credit. This token is redeemed on demand for any token on offer by an economic agent.

---

[139] On claims to 'fundamental value,' see esp. Chapter 12.3 and Appendices 5.1 and 12.2.
[140] Each staking contract will specify its particular version of these participation rights.

- *Commodity tokens.* These are issued by an economic agent on completion of an exchange. The token represents a right to the specific output (the 'underlier' it describes). It also generates a set of information associated with the exchange that forms the basis of data-rich economic performances that themselves generate new commodities.

Each will be considered in turn, both diagrammatically and with text. Figure 10.1 contains the visual elements that are components of all diagrams.

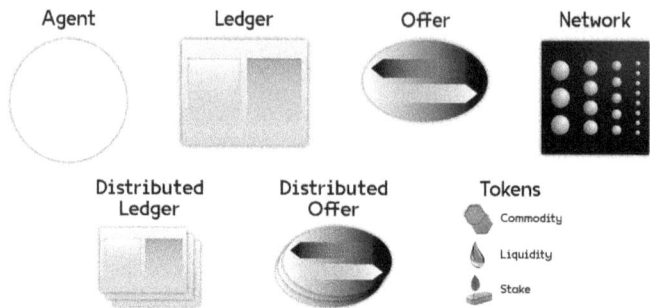

Figure 10.1 Visual elements representation legend

10.2 Stake tokens

Stake involves asset ownership capacities of participation in performances and exposure to dividends (yields) on performances. Reciprocal staking is a two-way economic communication interface, through which credit, commodities or other stake can be distributed throughout the network. As a process, reciprocal staking binds the network in on-going common interest. Stake tokens, issued to represent the transferred ownership of stake, perform the following roles:

- *Sharing the risks.* Risks of asset ownership have both an upside and downside. A transfer of stake involves one agent's acquisition of a share in the performance of another agent for purposes of both:
  » short stake-diversification positions. As each purchase of a stake token requires an issuance of stake by that purchaser, there is a hedging process for all agents to diversify their own risks, generating liquidity in the stake market.

» long performance-focusses positions. This could be called 'commitment staking.' Agents invest stake in those agents whose performances are likely to create future value in the network.[141]
- *Providing collateral for credit.* This enables shared liquidity. Stake-as-collateral means an agent can secure access to credit (liquidity) without having to exit their stake position.
- *Offers and dividends.* Stake tokens give the right to nodes in the network to receive offers from an issuer and, most importantly, to receive dividends.

Stake tokens have the following attributes:

- They are issued and accepted by agents in return for the stakes of others.
- They are financial positions on the future and a means to diversify the risks of ownership.
- They are a measurement of the aggregate performance of an economic agent.
- Their price is measured in the unit of exchange, and is reflected in the matched exchange offers. That price will reflect the valuation of the asset being staked, and will change broadly in relation to that valuation.
- They give voice to agents' decisions about what constitutes 'value' and where in the network it is best being created.
- They create performance data about the state of the economy.

The stake issuance process is shown in Figures 10.2 to 10.4.

Figure 10.2 Agent A publishes stake exchange offer to the network, proposing 500B for 900A

---

141 Readers who see this proposition as reminiscent of Keyne's critique of stock market speculation (trades motivated by 'other people's opinions') are invited to see Appendix 12.3.

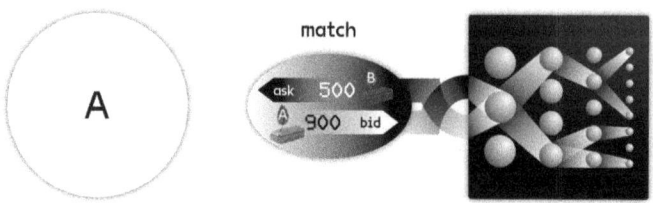

Figure 10.3 The network matches A's stake exchange offer

Figure 10.4 Agent A holds 500B and the network holds 900A

10.3 Liquidity tokens

In a distributed economy the offer-as-line-of-credit is the starting point and reciprocal token issuance is its appearance.[142] In exchange, when the offer is published, it becomes a line of credit, whether it be in the form of commodity credit (an offer to deliver output in the future) or financial credit (an offer of liquidity). Hence the offer stands as an option on credit proper. The right to exercise the option – to draw down on the line of credit by accepting the offer of credit – is itself a form of liquidity. In summary, the offer is liquidity, and the matching of that offer brings the liquidity token into being.

The incentive to issue liquidity tokens is the recognition that scaling transactions and complex networks will not work without intertemporal smoothing. This frames liquidity token offers as a social act of reciprocity: a contribution to keeping the wheels of commerce turning.

The Economic Space Protocol implements a 'network credit agreement' (with stake as collateral). A credit agreement is an automated 'topping up' of credit: when any credit is cleared by an act of exchange of

---

142 Economic textbooks want to explain money via a logical evolution from barter, and the growing complexity of economic transactions enabled by money. Anthropologists are inclined to emphasize the origins of trade in credit and the gift, bringing focus to the time interval in trade.

PROTOCOLS FOR POSTCAPITALIST EXPRESSION

liquidity tokens, the line of credit is topped up to its agreed limit. This ensures that credit offers are a constantly-adjusting stock, enabling credit itself to manifest as a flow. Credit tokens bear no interest or yield; nor are they an effective store of value.[143]

Liquidity tokens have the following attributes. They:

- Are denominated in the unit of exchange: credit clearing may only occur across entities of the same kind and denomination. In effect, liquidity tokens bring the unit of exchange to life as more than a passive numeraire mediating the valuation of other tokens: it becomes *a unit of distributed issuance of credit*.
- Come into being through a collateralized credit agreement. This means credit issuance effectively appears as automated.
- Are cleared when they serve an exchange. This is through netting by the distributed offer matching algorithm.
- Give a right to be redeemed on demand for any output on offer by the issuing economic agent, or to clear outstanding credit in the opposite direction.
- Are not held longer than necessary to settle a trade.

Credit relationships will be of two general types:

- *Credit issuance*. This is token issuance between agents directly involved in exchange of commodities or stake, giving the liquidity required to initiate exchange. This credit will generally be initiated to bring an act of production into being; for example to enable a producer to acquire inputs. It is presented diagrammatically as a *credit granting exchange offer*, represented in Figures 10.5 to 10.7.
- *Distributed clearing*. This token issuance is generated 'automatically' in the netting process, to enable an intertemporal match. It is automatically closed out once the ledger is settled. It is presented diagrammatically as a *credit clearing exchange offer*, represented in Figures 10.8 to 10.10

---

[143] Credit tokens are not designed to store value; indeed with no yield, their main risk is downside: the risk of default of the issuer. Default would be the event of the issuer not being able to provide/create its outputs, and not necessarily because of insolvency. For as long as an issuing agent creates value, the markets will adjust both the price of the offer and the reputation rating of the agent, indeed to the point that the agent may be no more than an issuer of credit. But as long as there is any demand for its commodity tokens, liquidity tokens will be matched until cleared.

Figure 10.5 An agent makes the network an (issuing credit) offer to exchange commodity X for liquidity tokens

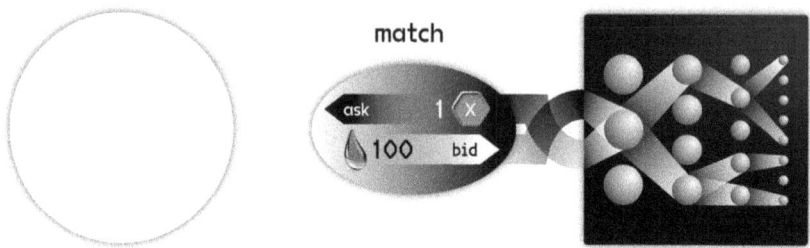

Figure 10.6 Network matches the offer, accepting liquidity tokens from agent

Figure 10.7 Network gives credit to the agent who now holds a liquidity token liability and a commodity token asset

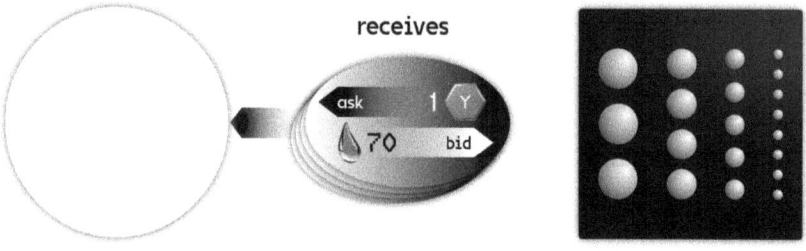

Figure 10.8 Agent receives a (clearing) offer from the network to exchange liquidity tokens for a commodity token

PROTOCOLS FOR POSTCAPITALIST EXPRESSION

Figure 10.9 Agent matches credit (clearing) offer

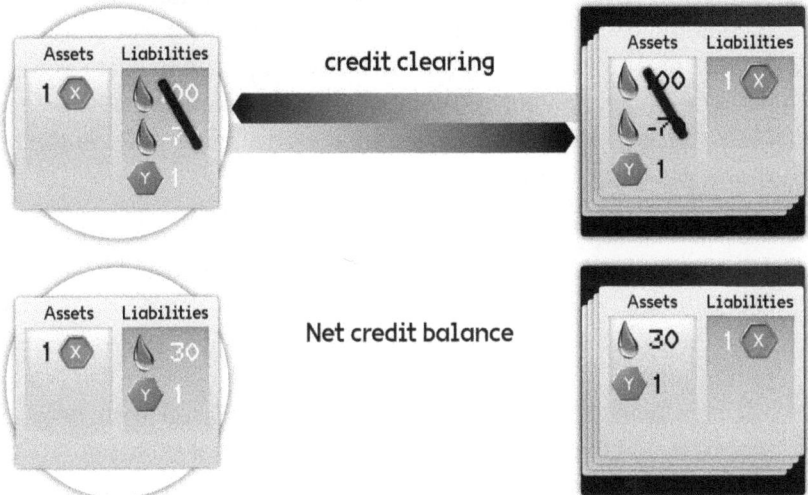

Figure 10.10 Agent's credit liabilities are cleared through netting, so the network now holds a net asset of 30 liquidity tokens

10.4 Commodity tokens

Economic agents initiate sales and purchases of goods and services. The tokens transacted in this process we call commodity tokens where the term 'commodity' means any good or service (tangible or intangible) produced for, and validated by, the network.[144]

In effect, the commodity token is designed to represent informational events that include, but are not limited to, the delivery of actual goods and service. In a single commodity exchange, price is just one data event, with the potential statistical significance of other data events awaiting discovery within the network. In a dynamic system of exchange,

---

144 See footnote 71 for our clarification of the use of the term 'commodity.'

commodity transactions will be tied to credit issuance. A commodity token, verifying the creation of commodity value, can be utilized to settle credit. Credit tokens and commodity tokens will therefore often be paired in clearing a ledger entry.

Each agent will be an issuer of its own commodity tokens and each commodity token offer attaches to a specific commodity output. The acceptance of the offer of a commodity, declared by issuance of a token in payment, means that every commodity has a matching token. Accordingly, the total of commodity tokens issued in a time period is equal to the total commodity exchange for that period. This is true for each individual agent and for the network as a total. When we separate the data into new commodities and re-circulated commodities, commodity token issuance can be used as a one proxy measure of a 'fundamental value' in the network (see Appendix 12.2).

Commodity tokens have the following attributes:

- Their quantity is determined by the offers/matches of individual agents.
- Their long-term price is determined by, and a measure of, the *real* output of an economic agent.
- They are priced through market offers, where the bid is the commodity token, and the ask is denominated in the unit of exchange.
- The risks of commodity production are carried by the direct producer; default risk is carried by the token holder.

Figures 10.11 to 10.13 depict commodity exchange.[145]

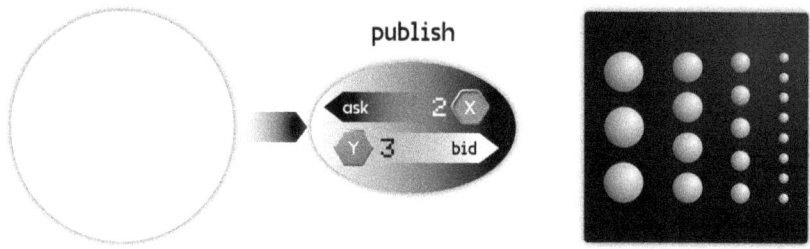

Figure 10.11 Agent publishes a commodity exchange offer

---

[145] Perry Mehrling's lectures on the 'Money view' make use of these types of diagrams. See http://sites.bu.edu/perry/.

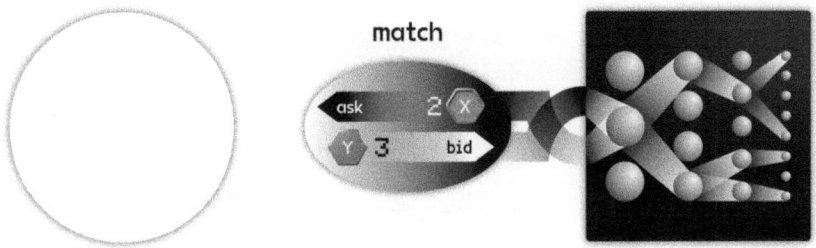

Figure 10.12 Network matches commodity exchange offer

Figure 10.13 Agent now has commodity X and network has commodity Y assets

10.5 Exchanges between tokens

The Economic Space Protocol sees different tokens having different roles in the network. But there will also be exchange relations across token types and a selection warrants particular note, as shown in Figure 10.4, to illustrate the meanings of cross-token transactions.

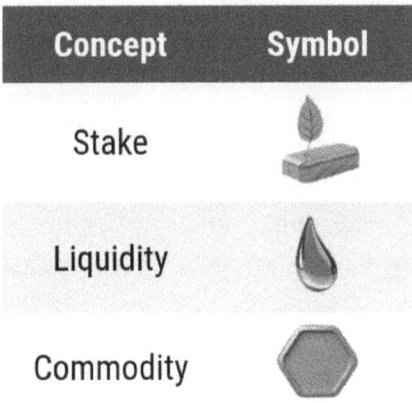

Figure 10.14 Cross-token exchanges

Agent A	Agent B	Operation Definition	Use
		Mutual stake holding creation	Entering shared risk positions / Creating liquidity / Appreciating relationship.
		Mutual stake holding dissolution	Exiting shared risk positions / Reducing liquidity / Depreciating or relocating relationship.
		Stake buying / selling	Issuer clearing debt by converting to stake. Shifts risk to stake holder.
		Stake transfer	Issuer selling stake to acquire liquidity, reducing risk. No net change in total network liquidity.
		Liquidity transfer	May occur automatically when an agent reduces a credit line with one agent, or increases a credit line with another.
		Distributed clearing	Occurs when the matching algorithm finds a path to clear credit across two or more parties to settle a trade.
		Credit issuance	Opens and extends trade time intervals. Exchanging a commodity for credit, to be redeemed later.
		Credit clearing	Closes the trade time interval. Credit is exchanged for a commodity, clearing previously issued credit.
		(Monetized) Barter	Exchange between two commodities with complete match: no time interval. Netting might be used, but without issuance of liquidity tokens.
		Stake on kind	Agent A exchanges its own commodity for a stake.
		In kind cash out	Used to simultaneously exit a risk position and purchase a commodity. It is the only way in which wealth can leave the network (as commodities).

Note: The cases above are post-netting trades. There may be one or more intermediate trades, or a combination of the above as the matching algorithm attempts to find offer matching routes.

Two simple points, among many, can be drawn from Figure 10.4. First, commodity tokens can be used for the acquisition of stake or other commodities, or they can be used to clear credit. The latter is the closest to a commodity token being thought of as 'money.' The network validation of an output does not generate cash, but the clearing of credit. Second, exogenous money (fiat or cryptocoins) can enter and leave the network as commodities. This means that fiat can be used indirectly for the purchase of stake or commodities or the clearing of credit, and commodity outputs can be conveyed to fiat. The exchange rate will be determined by offers on the network, and this will regulate the incentives to move assets between fiat and the Economic Space Protocol unit of exchange.

10.6 Three token categories to serve three economic functions

Figures 10.2 to 10.13 show sequences of token exchanges across token categories (commodity for credit, for example) as well as within token categories (for example commodity for commodity). We see in these diagrams that each token type plays a different role in the flow of assets in the network. Each token type holds, encoded in its programming as a financial instrument (i.e. a smart contract), certain rights that are distinct. Each token type serves a different purpose. In summary:

- *Stake tokens are shares of an economic agent's output.* They give the user the capacity to receive dividends through their application programming interface (API). It is an expression of accumulated ownership. Its ledger entry records a stock, and the attached exposure to the risks of growth and contraction in the value of that stock.[146] Furthermore, stake tokens serve as communication pipes, utilized for agents' economic peering.
- *Liquidity tokens grant the right to clear.* This right can be verified through their AIP. If a clearance is successful, a liquidity token with any remainder is returned. It is an exposure to future potential states, but without carrying the risks of those states (except for default). It involves the advancement (and writing down) of credit to meet the immediate liquidity requirements of the network, both those between

---

146 Flows of stake in a secondary market occur via commodity tokens, where stake is now a 'commodity' to be exchanged.

agents to maintain their accumulation and the matching and netting requirements of achieving settlement in exchange.
- *Commodity tokens are an exposure to an offer for an agreed output.* They are the most programmable token type, and can hold any interaction logic and carry any given rights. It comes into being only at the completion of a match, as verification of 'what already is.' This enables it to connect to measures of fundamental value as a 'real abstraction.'

It is only with these three token types (and the reciprocal flows they stand for, that the Economic Space Protocol is able to articulate a self-reproducing economic system.

CHAPTER 11

DYNAMICS OF A TOKENIZED NETWORK

11.1 Three circuits of value

The Economic Space Protocol is styled to give precision to the roles of different tokens, but there is a need to show how these token types, and the economic processes they express, relate together in the social process of 'value in movement.'[147] In this chapter we explore the economy in the style of a circular flow. This style depicts the economy as a sequence of critical inter-connections, located in space time, that combine to secure the conditions for the reproduction of the flow. A circular flow should not depict the protocol as a closed system (there can be interaction with capitalist markets at any point). Nor should the flow be presumed automatic. Any break in the flow is a possible interruption to the system, but they should be presumed and incorporated.

Nonetheless, the definition of a sustainable network is that it has the capacity to generate its own conditions of reproduction. Put simply, if the network requires continuous injections of outside money in order to reproduce (after an initial bootstrapping phase as described in Appendix 1.2), it cannot have aspirations of being a protocol on which to build a postcapitalist economy. Yet that should not gainsay the expectation that outside money *will* enter the network; but it will do so as a commodity, not as 'money,' and it will be to expand the network, not reproduce it.

Framing an economy as a circular flow has a long history in economics, starting most prominently from François Quesnay's *Tableau Économique*

---

147 Marx (1885: ch.4), described capital as a social relation of value:

> It is a movement, a circulatory process through different stages, which itself in turn includes three different forms of the circulatory process. Hence it can only be grasped as a movement, not as a static thing.

(1758), through Marx's circuits of capital in Volume II of *Capital* (1885) (explicitly connected by Marx to Quesnay), Luxemburg's *Accumulation of Capital* (1913), Sraffa's *Production of Commodities by Means of Commodities* (1960), Leontiev's input-output model (1966) and interpretations of Keynesian multiplier effects (sometimes said to have been derived from Marx). None of these depictions could be called a 'formal model,' at least not in the current sense in which that term is applied, but they are designed to be quantifiable (in a way that so much current discussion of the 'circular economy' is not). Our exposition here is conceived in that long tradition and offers a heuristic device to show patterns of inter-connectedness (and possible disconnection) in the economy.

We take our mode of exposition from Marx's (1885, Part I) depiction of circuits of capital. For Marx, these components of the circuit are money capital, commodity capital and industrial capital. All can be thought of as essential elements of a self-reproducing system, but they are also three ways of looking at an overall circular process that involves all of money, industry and commodities.[148]

In our depiction, the stages of the circular flow are: performance (Pe), collateral (Co) and credit (Cr). All circuits require each of these components. As a circuit, there is no original starting or end point, but when we describe the circuit by starting an explanation from each different point, and look at the way in which the circuit reproduces that nominated starting point, different issues of emphasis become prominent.

So we define:

- *The Performance Circuit (Pe–Co–Cr–Pe)*. This circuit describes the requirements for a performance to be reproduced (which must include not just the act of performing, but also the validation of those performances by the network – a process we refer to, for shorthand, as 'production and consumption').
- *The Collateral Circuit (Co–Cr–Pe–Co)*. This circuit describes the requirements for collateral to be reproduced (which must include the reproduction of the stake portfolio that forms the basis of collateral).

---

148 Marx saw these circuits as describing the path of individual companies and also the economy as a whole. The latter would be seen as a set of intersecting circuits where the output of one company is the input of another; the money revenue of one industrial process is shifted to fund another, etc.. These intersections are the focus of Leontiev's input-output analysis. We will not extend our analysis in this way, but it is consistent with that project.

PROTOCOLS FOR POSTCAPITALIST EXPRESSION

- *The Credit Circuit (Cr–Pe–Co–Cr)*. This circuit describes the requirements for network credit to be reproduced (which must include the process of credit clearing from the previous 'round' of credit).

Figure 11.1 shows a circuit in the new economic space. The outer ring is the 'real' economy of the flow between performances, collateral and credit. The inner circle shows the reciprocal token movements of commodity tokens, stake tokens and liquidity tokens. Consistent with our explanation of tokens and ledgers (Chapter 10), the 'real' processes flow in one direction (clockwise) and their reciprocal token issuance flows in the opposite direction (anticlockwise).

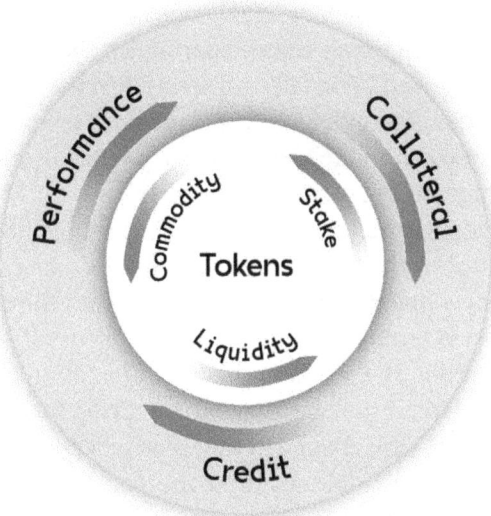

Figure 11.1 Circuits in the New Economic Space

11.2 The performance circuit: the circuit of value creation

The start and end point of this circuit focuses on production and consumption as a pairing, for combined they depict the performance of value creation in the network.

A performance starts with an offer by an agent to the network to produce outputs it believes will be valued by the network. The offer is also seeking staking from other agents who may directly participate or

163

take some financial interest in realizing the performance. Through staking, performances become (underlying) assets which is the key to their standing as collateral (Pe–Co).

The act of staking highlights that the offer of a performance is a risk position on the future: an estimation of whether the performance being staked will receive future social recognition (replication, adoption or some other form of socially recognized approval). This risk position is played out over time: whether a performance does, indeed, create the value its implementers intended and its stakers aspired to. The direct expression of the playing out of risk is the changing price of stake, as the network monitors the enactment of a performance.

When stake is used as collateral for credit issuance (Co–Cr), a change in the value of a performance, and hence of stake, means that the value of collateral will change over time. In particular, there is a risk that a performance whose staked value falls will see a fall in the value of collateral, and hence shift the risks of default to the issuer of credit. There will be clear incentives for collateral to be based on a pooling of staked performances. This is the momentum of 'risking together.'

Hence, when credit is used to fund the acquisition of inputs for the agent's next performance (be it repeating the same performance or innovating a new one) (Cr–Pe), it is apparent that the playing out of risks of the previous circuit impacts on the capacity of this agent to mobilize future credit. The signal of that risk evaluation is stake price. Stake framed as collateral now becomes the backing for the offer of a line of credit (Co–Cr), so the change in the value of a performance impacts the future provision of credit to fund the construction of future performances (Cr–Pe).

When framed as the circuit of an individual performance, we see emphasis on risks and changing network valuation of performances. When framed as the circuit of the total of network performances, we see how the growth of network-created value leads to the funding of new performances. Hence we depict Pe–Pe as the circuit of value creation.[149]

---

149 In the Marxian circuit, the return to the 'starting point' designates expanded value, acquired by the extraction of surplus value from labor. In our terms it would be a Pe–Pe circuit. But in the circuit of the new economic space, there is no process of surplus extraction from producers, so the circuit's growth is via replication, not extraction.

11.3 The collateral circuit: the circuit of growth

The start and end point of this circuit focuses on the propensity of the network to expand wealth. Wealth in the network is expressed in stake price growth, for staking, and hence stake price, responds to where new value is being created. But our analysis of a circuit – a flow – should not be centered on the stock dimension. This is why we focus on stake-as-collateral rather than stake-as-wealth.

Collateral is stake, qualified by risk, and measured by the unit of exchange. Stake exists as a (diversified) portfolio of unique, differentiated assets. When looked at as collateral, the focus shifts from the diversity of performance-backed stakes to the singularity of an abstracted unit of measure, expressed in the unit of exchange/unit of credit. Portfolio valuation is a critical analytical shift, for it opens up the calculative basis for decisions 'rebalancing' portfolio holdings as risks change. The intentional shift of agents' stake holdings is the key to shifting the growth and direction of the network.[150]

In summary, collateral is the conversion of a diverse range of stakeholdings into a single index of valuation, and from here it can be expressed in the same terms as credit (Co–Cr): from the perspective of the portfolio it is the unit of exchange; from the perspective of credit, it is the unit of credit. But it is the same unit.

Credit backed by collateral then appears as a trusted (risk-rated) source of liquidity, which will be advanced to individual agents to fund specific performances (Cr–Pe). In the previous link (Co–Cr), what was a process of converting diversity to sameness now becomes the opportunity for creating diversity out of sameness (Cr–Pe). This pulse from diversity to singularity to diversity drives the growth of the network. The question the circuit resolves is whether the performances that backed collateral at the 'start' of the circuit will be the same as the performances that get funded by the credit raised from the staking of those performances.

In this role, collateral is the means to make risk commensurable across the network so that different performances and their risk/return calculations can be expressed in a common unit of measure. The movement from Pe–Co, which completes the circuit, has expressed a view about which performances will thrive and which will not.

---

[150] 'Modern portfolio theory' tells us that the value of the whole is not simply found in adding up component prices: the composite risk profile impacts valuation.

The Co–Co circuit expresses the risk-adjusted measure of *growth of accumulation* by the network (compared with the Pe–Pe circuit which expresses the *growth of output value* of the network).

11.4 The credit circuit: the circuit of stability

The start and end point of this circuit focuses on the provision of liquidity and the propensity of the network to be stable (whilst it grows). Its starting point is individual offers of liquidity to enable the network's new value creation (production and consumption). An agent draws on credit to fund the design, build and stake a future performance (Cr–Pe). The provision of credit avoids illiquidity which would otherwise impede the creation of (stakeable) performances. From the perspective of the credit circuit, the movement Cr–Pe expresses the decision about *which* performances will be staked: which performances are most likely to succeed, and hence repay the credit from the value of their outputs.

The movement Pe–Co reveals that the risks of the creditor and staker are different. The staker's risk is reflected in their dividend deriving from the value of the performance. It is the *growth* position. The creditor's risk is simply that the performance generates enough return on stake to give the issuer of stake tokens sufficient revenue to repay credit. This is both a lower level of risk so credit will more likely be directed towards 'safer' investments: riskier investments will likely rely more on stake than on credit. This is the sense in which the credit circuit emphasizes the capacity of the system for stability.

When the circuit is completed by collateral as the backing for credit (Co-Cr), it is now apparent that the more successful stakes are the ones that 'survive' to form future collateral, and especially collateral that will not decline in value over the life of the circuit. This selection process establishes a stable basis on which further performances can be chosen and funded.

When framed as the circuit of an individual line of credit, the circuit shows the processes by which the conditions for its repayment are created (and the risks that are 'passed through the circuit). When framed as the circuit of total credit we see how credit is being directed to those performances most likely to meet risk/return calculus. The credit circuit, therefore signals not just the stability of the circuit, but the stability of the connection over time between performances and value.

11.5 Significance

The circuits described above are a heuristic device: they are not inputs into a model or input/output analysis of the new economic space. The objective is to show that a single transaction, posed as a movement in a circuit, takes on different meaning according to how the circuit is being described. This is more than a statement that, to invoke Gunnar Myrdal, all points of view are views from a point (although that is important). It is that these different meanings form a spread of meaning, and therein lies fertile grounds for volatility in the system. But it is not a volatility to be eradicated as a threat; indeed it is the lifeblood of the network. Without volatility, the system would stagnate.

CHAPTER 12

STABILITY, VOLATILITY AND VALUE

12.1 Stability

In a distributed protocol, claims to stability cannot relate to conventional macroeconomic indicators like unemployment and GDP growth, nor to counter-cyclical policy measures. Those agendas are tasked to states: their taxing and expenditure policies and their monetary regulation capacities. Instead, claims to stability must be about the relationship between tokens and the material underliers of the network. To claim more – for example, to maintain stability with respect to the US dollar or to US economic growth – is not just a claim that, in practice, cannot be sustained (at least not without making this the sole purpose of a token); it is an aspiration we do not hold. A different economy, with a different set of goals and processes, is intended to diverge from the US economy; not to track its performance. This relates to our proposal that participants in the new economic space, who nonetheless remain heavily exposed to capitalist economies, will be 'living in the spread' (Chapter 1.6). The centrality of tokens in the Economic Space Protocol relates to token value stability and the capacity of tokens to facilitate economic processes in ways that tie token issuance to 'real' value and the capacity of credit issuance to the smooth operation of the network.

We have the opportunity to rethink what we mean by stability. An economy may be stable in its own terms: its average return on capital, unemployment rate and exchange rate may be stable (we once could have included inflation rate and interest rates here; but no longer), but it may be unstable by other criteria such as poverty levels, life expectancy, access to health care, housing affordability or carbon emissions. When targeted metrics of a postcapitalist economy are different from those of a capitalist economy, each economy will likely appear as volatile, if not failing, when measured by the metrics of the other. We believe that the most robust claims of 'stability' cannot rest on attachment to another entity itself deemed 'stable,' without becoming a mere replica of that other entity. Stability must be a statement about self; not others. The claims to stability of the new economy are threefold:

The unit of exchange/unit of credit stabilizes as the economy scales. This means the network is trusting the relationship between the credit and the network's system of output valuation: in effect, new value created in the network is an accepted means to clear credit in the network.

Stake prices change in an orderly way. This means that stake price reflects 'fundamental value' and the economy is producing the output it claims to produce.

Volatility inside the network is a statement about the relationship between stake prices and the unit of exchange. This gives a measure of stability/volatility of 'real' network change over time and applies to both the volatility of individual stake prices and the total value of stake in the network.

12.2 Outside currency within the network

A further issue of stability comes when we consider the impact of outside money within the network.[151] There is nothing stopping agents exchanging in dollars, just as they can use any object – a bag of barley or a coat – as a particular unit of exchange. But these will have to convert to other units for recognition across the network.

It has been mentioned (e.g. Chapter 10.5) that dollars can enter the network, but they do so as commodities, not as token substitutes. Entering as a commodity means that something must be 'given up' (offers of commodities or stake expressed in terms of the network unit of exchange) to acquire dollars. Nonetheless, a commodity entry of dollars does create an implicit exchange rate between the protocol unit of exchange and the dollar, for commodities and stake can be priced in either. Nonetheless, the entry of dollars and the creation of an exchange rate has significance. First, the exchange rate will impact where agents source commodities and how they fund stake, indicating that there are no clear boundaries to the network. This is the money/token dimension of living in the spread. Second, the exchange rate between the unit of exchange of the Economic Space Protocol and the dollar will likely be volatile. This doesn't challenge the stability of the unit of exchange within

---

[151] Outside money (Gurley and Shaw, 1960) could be fiat currencies or other forms like bitcoin. For simplicity we will represent outside money as ' dollars.'

the new economy's token system; indeed, over time, the question will be whether it is the network's unit of exchange or the dollar which is to be described as 'volatile.' In that optimistic statement lies the expression of the political battle for legitimacy of the new economic space.

12.3 Volatility

With stability defined by reference to the value of outputs in the new economic space (see Appendix 12.2), there is no juxtaposition of stability and volatility. The goal is not to reduce volatility in the name of stability, but to recognize that volatility is integral to financial markets and to risk. The goal is to direct volatility and see that it occurs in parts of the system where there is 'intentional' indeterminacy; where it expresses flexibility, discovery and the estimation of risk and of value. Agents creating performances, purchasing stake, and changing their minds about which performances are value-creating, will generate welcome volatility as the pulse of the new economy. Each of these can be thought of as financial spreads, in which agents take positions.

So volatility can be both essential to dynamism and itself convey valuable information. We know that in conventional capital markets, the development and trading of real-time volatility indices is seen as a critical market indicator. Inside a volatile market there are standard strategies for hedging to neutralize volatility ('delta hedging') and, moreover, to profit from trading volatility itself, stripped of directionality (Lee, 2020).

We are not seeking to initiate the development of volatility-trading markets in the Economic Space Protocol (though nor do we hold a view as to the likelihood or merits of their development). The emergence of DeFi opens significant potential for these markets. Yet for all the potential of DeFi, it is currently just replicating the calculus of mainstream finance. While adding flexibility and capacity to agents, it also has potential of leveraging instability for its own sake.

There are (as yet) no techniques for modeling current volatility in crypto markets. Any suggestion that DeFi can offer a cryptoeconomy financial tools to accurately measure (and hence delta hedge) volatility should be treated skeptically. Volatility is an expression not just of inefficiency of estimation but of social dynamics expressed in financial channels. Managing the channels does not itself stabilize social dynamics: it causes volatility to displace into other modes of expression. So for the Economic Space Protocol, there is no intention to control volatility with the goal of restricting it, but to direct it to sites where it can be embraced (as potential). Accordingly, volatility has two central roles.

First, the information generated in markets has to be interrogated for patterns that can be given economic meanings as 'performances': offers of data analytics. Volatility here will be associated with the issuance of stake in those performances. But such performances carry risks, there can be no certainty about which performance designs will generate information which is valued by the network.[152] For any particular performance, this source of volatility can be expected to diminish as the performance becomes statistically consolidated; with new performances continually being configured, the domain of the issuance of stake itself remains an on-going site of volatility.

Secondly, the value of staked positions will change constantly as agents change their views about what performances are successful (valuable). This will be a domain of continual volatility, for volatility is the condition of liquidity in the market for stakes.

It will be apparent that, in practice, the two volatilities will not be discrete: the first will embed expectations about the second, and the second will reflect levels of confidence in the first. The network has capacity to trace which economic events are associated with which stake price changes. This can be thought of as feedback loops on performance staking, vetting the values of past performance designs and giving incentives for agents to design more precise/granular performances.

These stability-generating loops offer no guarantees of the network being long-run stable in its outcomes on the terms we have nominated. We should not overstate the capacity for creating stable outcomes. History shows that guarantees of stable systems only come with authoritarian control, and then only for as long as resistance can be suppressed.

Currently, nation states, for all their regulatory and legal enforcement capacities, are struggling to secure even modest economic stability. For those states, policies for stabilization must be reconciled with a politics of whose interests have been served by the instability, whose interests must be protected in any stabilization process, and hence who is going to absorb the costs of stabilization policies. Moreover, this playing out of deep conflicts has to all be wrapped in a policy discourse of economic necessity and common interest, while in fact being neither of those.

---

152 In effect, the distinction between 'noise' and 'real information' (Black, 1986) cannot be known in advance.

We are not engaging in this same process. Although we describe the network as a commitment to a collective future, especially through reciprocal staking and the mechanisms of distributed credit, there is no suggestion that this is the playing out of a single, agreed vision. Protocols are about processes, not realizing a pre-given agenda. Our goal is that in creating the conditions for a collective future, divided aspirations have transparent expression and network conflicts have mechanisms to be played out in an orderly way; not hidden behind the idea that a centralized authority knows and implements the common good.

APPENDIX 12.1

TOKENIZED VALUE: SIMPLE AND EXPANDED

Marx drew the distinction between the simple form of value (the exchange of commodities) and the general form of value (growth, or the accumulation of capital). Keynes drew a roughly similar distinction between a 'real exchange economy' (monetized barter) and a 'monetary economy' (which includes time, credit, liquidity and therefore risk) (see Appendix 8.1). How do we describe tokens in the expanded accumulation of a 'monetary economy'?

Each performance is itself (in combination with other performances) eventually revealed in the creation of commodities.[153] It could be a 'conventional' commodity (good or service) but performances have been framed in the Economic Space Protocol to engage also data commodities, or what we have called economic media. This focus represents what is distinctive about commodities in the 21st century compared with the eras of both Marx and Keynes: the rise to prominence of intangible outputs whose value-as-commodity is so difficult to specify (see Appendix 5.1).

In order to gain analytical access to data commodities, we have brought stake (and its projections of a contingent future of the performance) to the center of the analysis. The proposition is that the outputs of performances themselves may be difficult to define and measure, but that every proposed output should be measured by its intended outcomes, and that these can be expressed in measurable ways. But the stark, consequential expression of output evaluation is the preparedness to stake the process of their creation, and this can be clearly measured in a market process. Perhaps, it might be said, shifting from commodities being exchanged (Marx, Keynes) to performances being staked, and referring to this as the 'simple' form of value, is stretching the word 'simple.' But, we believe, this is necessary as a way of recognising the prominence of information in commodity-money relations.

---

153 Despite reference here to Marx, our use of the term 'commodity,' explained in footnote 71.

The expanded form of value in our analysis is qualitatively different from what we depict as the simple form, and the critical difference remains centered on the role of information. In this expanded version, information is not just the means by which individual agents make decisions about the future (what to stake). It is also the means by which the collective of agents (the network) reaches its determination of what constitutes value. For both Marx and Keynes, the rule of profit is central to delineating what parts of the economy grow via a cycle of profit and investment, and what parts shrink. For them, what constitutes 'value' is a resolved parameter, defined by the protocols that constitute capitalist accumulation. But in the new economic space, without a predetermined measure of 'value,' expansion becomes a more fluid process, for when agents stake performances, they not only project its creative success on a two dimensional scale (how profitable it will be) but now also on a third dimension (what will be judged socially to be valuable). In this framing, reading trends (information) is the universal key to explaining the dynamics of value.

APPENDIX 12.2

MV=PQ: AN APPLICATION TO THE ECONOMIC SPACE PROTOCOL TOKEN LOGIC

The claim that the new economic space is grounded in fundamental value has been made on multiple occasions. It is perhaps a contentious one, predominantly because the concept itself is contentious.

Many economists balk at the concept of 'fundamental value.' Some do so because they believe that current price in the market is a sufficient measure of 'value' and any idea that value is something 'deeper' than price, as the classical economists believe, is simply metaphysics. Hayek and the neo-classical economists are disposed to this view. Others, in the tradition of Keynes, (also) reject fundamental value specifically as it relates to asset prices. Asset prices, they say, incorporate guesses about the future expressed in the present and, as no-one can know the future, asset prices now are just expressions of popular opinion about the future (see Appendix 5.1).

The Economic Space Protocol generates a direct connection between tokens and their material foundations in the 'real' economy. This foundation is what we mean by fundamental value: it implies a mode of valuing that looks to 'deeper' determinants (underliers) and discounts for speculation and short-term price movements. A clear connection between tokens and their underliers is itself a claim to a critical form of stability within the network.

In cryptoeconomics, there emerged significant engagement with the concept of fundamental value, including via options pricing theory and the efficient markets hypothesis. We have made contributions to this debate in the past (e.g. Bryan 2018). Much analysis involves application of the old (originally 18th century; attributed to philosopher David Hume) 'equation of exchange,' often expressed as the 'quantity theory of money.' The Economic Space Protocol can give a version of a quantity theory as a way of verifying the direct connection of tokens to underliers at both the level of individual transactions and the level of the network overall.

The formula of the old Quantity Theory of Money states: MV=PQ. Where:

M = the quantity of money in circulation,

V = its velocity of circulation of money,

P = the general price level in the economy and

Q = the quantity of goods and services sold in the economy.

The cryptoeconomics discussion of this issue has been innovative and creative, albeit that interest in it appears to have fallen away in the past few years, despite the growing popularity of terms like 'creator economy' and 'ownership economy' which suggest the generation of measurable value.

Taking MV=PQ into a crypto setting has required each of the variables be significantly adapted.Tokens are not simply 'M,' and hence V must change meaning (velocity of what?). In the Economic Space Protocol, 'P' is not a mono-measure of the terms of exchange and hence Q cannot be adequately expressed in relation to P.

A token only comes into existence when an offer is matched (and expressed through the creation of a debit and a credit record on corresponding ledgers). As an aggregate, we can compile a list of offers. Thus an offer expresses the potential creation (supply) of a token. An exchange offer between a good or service(Q), and a token instrument(M), where Q units are in the bid and M units are in the ask, denotes the exchange ratio relationship between Q and M, that can be interpreted as the price (P) of a Q unit, in terms of M. V is the speed at which M is issued and cleared; an issue of liquidity considered Chapter 9.

M represents the number of token units required to fulfill that exchange (Potential M). Since M is revolving, meaning it flows in both directions (as it is both 'earned' and 'spent') we can say that V is the average speed at which M flows in both directions in a given period of time. V then constitutes a multiplier where a net revolving amount of M, is required to fulfill all offers of Q at price P. Thus $M \times V = \sum(PM \times Q)$ (per period of time used to calculate V) .

Where Q1P1 can be matched with Q2P2, netting represents an instant exchange, or it could be said that the M component can be netted away.

The distributed market processes of offers and matching, closed by a netting process, gives a literal interpretation/verification of MV=PQ. Because every token offer (potential M) must be matched by a 'commodity' (PQ) in order to become 'actual' M, then M and PQ are '2 sides of the same token offer.' And in this context, with every match the M that is specific to it expires. New M comes into being with a new offer validated by its matching. In effect, the velocity of a token is infinite, so M tends towards 0: that is, the settlement of an exchange is at once the expiry of M. There is money flow, but no money *supply* required: M can be deemed to have been simultaneously issued and redeemed. So MV=PQ is definitionaly true, albeit not quite as an identity (as it is in the quantity theory of money), but as a protocol design.

The above depiction, making a clear and direct connection of tokens to output, is contingent upon a direct offer matching and complete netting. The introduction of a time interval (credit) and the possibility that matching may be indirect, or mediated through a web of matchings, requires a deeper explanation.

Netting is not itself an explanation of fundamental value when trades occur at different times and there is not a one-to-one correspondence between offers. Put simply, netting presupposes the existence of the things to be netted, yet their delivery to market will not be simultaneous with the offer. Temporal gaps open a need for credit to provide liquidity to the time interval. Hence fundamental value must be explained in the context of credit and the need to create liquidity across a time interval. In this context, credit itself has fundamental value: delivery on its promise of future exchangeability.

CHAPTER 13

THE CONDITIONS OF A DIGITAL POSTCAPITALIST ECONOMY

13.1 Introduction

The Economic Space Protocol proposes an economy of distributed relations, without reliance on a central 3rd party authority. This is not a proposition that current nation states are redundant, for there are many centralized facets of society, and the rule of law is a conspicuous one, which impact directly on the economy. The new economy will exist in any foreseeable future within a mainstream social and economic context. It is simply presenting an alternative economic way of being and doing, and it offers a protocol that can be readily adopted by anyone, without the sponsorship of any nation-state.

How the new economy interfaces with the conventional economy is an open design space, but also a domain of uncertainty. The specific objective of our analysis is to present the case, and it can be no more than a case, that, after an initial bootstrapping phase, the Economic Space Protocol offers a set of economic relations that can be self-reproducing. There will be porous boundaries between the conventional economy and the new economy: fiat money, commodities and people will move between the two systems. Indeed it is likely that every single user will have a foot in each system. But it is critical that we can present an economic logic for a coherent alternative that can become independent of constant financial top-up from outside (for example in dollars). A design goal is that the new economy can produce a surplus that generates its own conditions of continuation and expansion.

Self-sustainability in a narrow economic sense is important, but it would be a modest achievement if the alternative we are proposing looks pretty much the same as the existing system. The new economic space we are proposing offers a new vision of economic relations: the conditions of increasing equality of living standards, the creation of environmental health, and an economy sensitive to the aesthetic, cultural, and emotional attachments of participants. These are the collectively-determined, socially-defined conceptions of calculable value creation, or what we can term simply 'network value.'

13.2 Network value

The contention throughout this analysis is the capacity of the new economic space to incorporate performances creating outputs motivated by network value, and the capacity of the network to reward the performances that animate network value creation. We need to make as clear as possible the connection between network value, rewards and system reproduction. It requires all elements of the Economic Space Protocol, and all the earlier chapters to be brought together.

Performances motivated by network value are already familiar: philanthropy, crowdfunding, etc. are all expressions of this agenda. The challenge is to show the conditions under which network value is sustained and reproduced without the need for continual injections of outside money. In other words, the social surplus recognized in network value needs to be seen as equivalent to profit in capitalism: where the market evaluates and rewards performances with a yield of some form recognized by the network, either through individual agents or the commons.

Outputs being 'recognized by the network' is the term we use rather than 'selling for a profit,' for many performances may not generate profit; indeed are not targeting that objective. But they are targeting *some* objective: we are not compiling the conditions where just any old performance might expect reward.

The 'yield,' if not profit, must be in a form acceptable to the network: it could be commodities, credit, stake or indeed any kind of governance or access rights. The condition of the network being capable of self-reproducing is that the yield takes a form that the network can use for its reproduction: the yield is, or can be converted to, the inputs required to open another circuit of accumulation. This capacity to form a circuit is critical to the difference from philanthropy, which requires on-going injections of outside money for a new circuit to commence.

The question remains: how does the network systematically recognize the values that animate performances, such that those values are recognized and reproduced by the circuit of accumulation? Here, the issue of staking is pivotal. The market-based determination of which performances agents are willing to stake is the network's way of declaring what sorts of outputs (and the notions of value they embed) the network is backing financially. If we assume that staking is undertaken for reward, as described above, it must be the case that the ways outputs get recognized by the network provide the conditions of reproduction of the circuit, including the remuneration of stake.

However, this is not a sufficient framing to complete the argument, for it is posed only in terms of the conditions of reproduction of individual stakes and individual outputs and their outcomes; not the network as a whole. The additional dimension relevant here is that stake is the collateral for credit, and credit is paid down out of both commodity token exchanges and rewards for performances. With a focus on the conditions of issuance and repayment of credit, the analysis takes the general form, expressed now in the network's unit of credit. The ultimate test of the network's embrace of network value, and outputs produced in accordance with that value calculus, is whether a commodity token, received in return for the provision of a particular commodity output, will be accepted by (all agents in) the network for purposes of clearing credit. Its acceptance is network verification; its denial is the opposite.

Acceptance will not be a sudden and arbitrary determination at the moment of offer, as the above depiction may seem to suggest. Information flows in the network, taking the form of performances (for data must be encoded with meaning), will be providing agents in the network with real-time information on how offers are being evaluated and matched. So, working backwards from the acceptance of a commodity token in paying down credit, we can identify the social logic that leads to its likelihood of acceptance: the commodity token must relate to a commodity deemed valuable, which must come from a performance deemed value-creating, which is funded by stake deemed by a critical number of staking agents to be an investment in value creation and deemed by the network as providing collateral worthy of credit issuance.

This is the general process by which the Economic Space Protocol supports and sustains an economy of network value. In the new economy, everything depends on everything else, as it does in a capitalist economy or any economic system. The taxonomies and measures, the systems of valuation and rewards and the pulses that keep the system moving are all mutually defining. It cannot be otherwise. At the core of the Economic Space Protocol is a simple proposition: in a distributed economy, everything depends on the generation and processing of agent-generated information, and the way that information is compiled, evaluated and acted on must also be agent-centered. So the Economic Space Protocol is a case for agent-centered internal credibility and coherence, and the condition of entry is the desire to experiment.

13.3 Where to from here?

The protocol design principles of the new economic space have required that we cover some detailed and diverse conceptual and philosophical issues and combine them with the capacities of programmable protocol design. There are, no doubt, other ways to imagine and initiate a transition to postcapitalism, and we welcome that debate.

The proposal presented here makes the case that the conditions of postcapitalism lie latent within capitalism and, to make that latent potential imminent, we must develop ways to engage capitalism at its contemporary frontier of innovation; to go beyond, rather than to turn back. In particular, we need to engage three related elements.

First is the emergence of a digital economy, which provides the technology to build that digital future, even though it is also integral to many of the incapacities of current capitalism to meet many social needs (notably well-paying 'jobs');

Second is the risks that people are currently experiencing in their individual and collective lives: most obviously the risks of individual financial precarity on the one hand, and environmental destruction on the other. We are not trying to eliminate risk: we want to initiate social and economic relations where people can choose to risk in the creation of new things, to do so in creative, cooperative ways, and to have those creations valued socially. This will include, but is not restricted to, risking to innovate to address issues of inequality and environmental destruction.

Third is the rise to economic and social dominance of a culture of financial calculation. Individually, this is expressed as the need for debt to acquire housing or gain education or, for too many, to undertake daily subsistence. This rise is integral to the current acceleration of a wide range of inequalities and poverties. Currently, this culture is expressed in the rise of banking and insurance as a site of both political power and economic crisis creation, but also a site of extraordinary innovation. We seek to take over that innovation.

So we have adapted the capacities of post-blockchain technologies for protocol design to create ways for people in a network to risk together using financial techniques of staking, derivatives, liquidity, volatility, etc.. We are creating an economic media for postcapitalism.

This innovation has required that we redesign elements of economic and social language and analysis. For some readers, this will have taken them through debates and specifications that felt excessively detailed, and perhaps even at points semantic, but we believe that language is important. The old categories always pull us back to old ways of posing and answering problems. Our project has seen us, over quite some time, imagining future economic possibilities and then having to configure the categories as well as the analysis that will bring them coherence. It has, we agree, made for a challenging read. Nonetheless, we are confident that, for all this analytical detail, when it comes to being part of the network and living in the performances it enables, the operational design can be quite simple.

To get to that stage, where people are living at least aspects of their lives in a new economic space, more development work will be needed. This document has intentionally left unaddressed how the new economic space has a financial bridge to the capital markets, and a full exploration of the 'outside spread' that will likely drive capital market engagement with the new economic space. These developments await responses to the current document.

These are complex, but solvable issues. They become solvable not because there is a decisive answer but because protocol design embeds indeterminacy, volatility and ambiguity. The question will be whether the Economic Space Protocol has embedded them in coherent ways that enable creative adaptation of agent practices and of the protocol itself. For now, we present the network as its own internal logic; as a way of depicting a viable, evolving, distributed postcapitalism, where participants design their own futures, both individually and collectively.

So we now invite feedback, debate and expressions of interest from diverse sources, but especially from people and their organizations who can see in this proposal new ways of addressing social problems they have always known, or who now sense a potential for change they could not previously have imagined possible.

BIBLIOGRAPHY

Agamben, G. 2011 *The Kingdom and the Glory. For a Genealogy of the Economy and Government.* Translated by Chiesa, L. with Mandarini, M. Stanford: Stanford University Press.

Austin, J.L. 1962 *How to Do Things with Words.* Oxford: Clarendon Press.

Ayache, E. 2008 'I am a creator,' *Wilmott Magazine.* https://www.yumpu.com/en/document/view/34270375/elie-ayache-ito-33

Bank of England 2014 'How is money created.' https://www.bankofengland.co.uk/knowledgebank/how-is-money-created.

Barlow, J.B. 1996 'A Declaration of the Independence of Cyberspace.' https://www.eff.org/cyberspace-independence

Baudrillard, J. 1976 *For a Critique of the Political Economy of the Sign.* Translated by Levin, C. New York: Telos Press.

Beller, J. 2021 *The World Computer: Derivative Conditions of Racial Capitalism.* Durham: Duke University Press.

Beller, J. 2017 *The Message is Murder: Substrates of Computational Capital.* London: Pluto Press.

Beller, J., Bryan, D., Lee, B., López, J. & Virtanen, A. 2020 'Rethinking Money and Credit in a Cryptoeconomy: Securing Liquidity without the Need for Central Control of Issuance.' A preprint prepared for 'MIT Cryptoeconomic Systems,' Issue 1. https://assets.pubpub.org/mqc2esfj/21581340206367.pdf

Benveniste, E. 1971 *Problems in General Linguistics.* Translated by Meek, M, and Cables, C. Miami: University of Miami Press.

Bergson, H. 1889 *Time and Free Will: An Essay on the Immediate Data of Consciousness.* English translation by Pogson, F. London: George Allen and Unwin, 1910.

Berardi, F. 2012 'Semiocapitalism and the problem of solidarity.' https://libcom.org/book/export/html/45057

Berardi, F. 2009 *The Soul at Work: From Alienation to Autonomy*. Translated by Cadel, F. and Mecchia, G. Los Angeles: Semiotexte.

Bernes, J. 2020 'Planning and anarchy,' *South Atlantic Quarterly*, Vol.119, No.1.

Black, F. 1986 'Noise,' *Journal of Finance*, Vol.4, No.3.

Boyer-Xambeau, M., Deleplace, G. and Gillard, L. 1994 *Private Money and Public Currencies: The Sixteenth Century Challenge*. Translated by Azodi, A. Armonk: M.E. Sharpe.

Brand Finance 2022 *Global Intangible Finance Tracker*, 2022. https://brandirectory.com/reports/gift-2022

Bryan, D. 2018 'Valuation crisis and crypto economy,' ECSA Economic Ideas, *Medium*, May 16. 'https://medium.com/econaut/valuation-crisis-and-crypto-economy-39c5b7e373af

Bryan, D., Lee, B., Wosnitzer, R. and Virtanen, A. 2018 'Economics back into cryptoeconomics,' ECSA Economic Ideas. *Medium*, September 18. https://medium.com/econaut/economics-back-into-cryptoeconomics-20471f5ceeea

Bryan, D. and Rafferty, M. 2006 *Capitalism with Derivatives: A Political Economy of Financial Derivatives, Capital and Class*. London: Palgrave Macmillan.

Bryer, R.A. 2000 'The history of accounting and the transition to capitalism in England, part 1: theory; part 2: evidence,' *Accounting, Organizations and Society* Vol.25, Nos.2&3.

Buterin, V. 2013 'Ethereum: A Next-Generation Smart Contract and Decentralized Application Platform' https://ethereum.org/669c9e2e2027310b6b3cdce6e1c52962/Ethereum_Whitepaper_-_Buterin_2014.pdf ; https://ethereum.org/en/whitepaper/.

Buterin, V. 2017 'The meaning of decentralization,' *Medium*, February 6. https://medium.com/@VitalikButerin/the-meaning-of-decentralization-a0c92b76a274

Callon, M. 2007 'What does it mean to say that economics is performative?,' in MacKenzie, D. Muniesa, F. and Siu, L. (eds) *Do Economists Make Markets? On the Performativity of Economics*. Princeton: Princeton University Press.

Chiapello, E. 2007 'Accounting and the birth of the notion of capitalism,' *Critical Perspectives on Accounting*, Vol.18. http://www.arikamayanti.lecture.ub.ac.id/files/2014/12/Accounting-and-the-Notion-of-Capitalism.pdf

Deleuze, G. 1988 *Bergsonism*. New York: Zone Books.

Deleuze, G. and Guattari, F. 1983 *Anti-Oedipus: Capitalism and Schizophrenia*. Minneapolis: University of Minnesota Press.

Deleuze, G. and Guattari, F. 1987 *A Thousand Plateaus: Capitalism and Schizophrenia*. Minneapolis: University of Minnesota Press.

Derman, E. 2002 'The perception of time, risk and return during periods of speculation.' https://papers.ssrn.com/sol3/papers.cfm?abstract_id=296401

Dixon, C. 2018 'Why decentralization matters,' *OneZero*, February 19. https://onezero.medium.com/why-decentralization-matters-5e3f-79f7638e.

Doepke, M. and Schneider M. 2013 'Money as a unit of account,' National Bureau of Economic Research, Working Paper 19537. http://www.nber.org/papers/w19537

Drumm, C. 2021 'The Difference that Money Makes: Sovereignty, Indecision, and the Politics of Liquidity.' University of California, Santa Cruz, Dissertation. https://www.proquest.com/openview/4c5929e-cd96d074231b9d386b509f472/1.pdf

ERights.Org, n.d. 'E-language: Secure distributed persistent language for capability-based smart-contracting.' http://www.erights.org/

Ehrsam, F. 2016 'Blockchain tokens and dawn of the decentralized business model.' Blog-post, August 1. https://fehrsam.xyz/blog/blockchain-tokens-and-the-dawn-of-the-decentralized-business-model

Elson, D. 1979 'The value theory of labour,' in Elson, D. (ed.) *Value: The Representation of Labour in Capitalism*. London: CSE Books and Humanities Press.

Fanti, G., Lipsky, J. and Moehr, O. 2022 'Central bankers' cybersecurity challenge,' *Finance and Development*, September. https://www.imf.org/en/Publications/fandd/issues/2022/09/Central-bankers-new-cybersecurity-challenge-Fanti-Lipsky-Mochr

Foucault, M. 1974 *The Order of Things. An Archeology of the Human Sciences*. New York: Pantheon.

Fleischman, T., Dini P. and Littera, G. 2020 'Liquidity-saving through obligation-clearing and mutual credit: An effective monetary innovation for SMEs in times of crisis,' *Journal of Risk and Financial Management*, Vol.13, Issue12. https://www.mdpi.com/1911-8074/13/12/295

Graeber, D. 2011 *Debt: The First 5,000 Years*. Brooklyn: Melville House.

Graham, B. and Dodd, D. 1934 *Security Analysis*. New York: McGraw-Hill.

Grigg, I. 2000 'Financial cryptography in 7 layers,' Proceedings of Financial Cryptography Fourth International Conference, Anguilla, British West Indies, February. https://iang.org/papers/fc7.html

Grigg, I. 2004 'The Ricardian contract.' https://iang.org/papers/ricardian_contract.html

Guattari F. 1992 *Chaosmosis: An Ethico-Aesthetic Paradigm*. Translated by Bains, P. and Pefanis, J. Bloomington and Indianapolis: Indiana University Press, 1995.

Gurley, J. and Shaw, E. 1960 *Money in a Theory of Finance*. Washington DC: The Brookings Institution.

Hardt, M. and Negri, A. 2000 *Empire*. Cambridge, Mass.: Harvard University Press.

Harney, S. and Moten. F. 2013 *The Undercommons: Fugitive Planning & Black Study*. London: Minor Compositions.

Hayek, F.A. 1941 *The Pure Theory of Capital*, London: Macmillan.

Hayek, F.A. 1944 *The Road to Serfdom*. Chicago: Chicago University Press.

Hayek, F.A. 1945 'The use of knowledge in society,' *American Economic Review*. Vol.XXXV, No.4.

Hayek, F.A. 1988 *The Fatal Conceit: The Errors of Socialism*. Chicago: Chicago University Press.

HM Treasury 2020 *The Magenta Book: Central Government Guidance on Evaluation*. March. https://www.gov.uk/government/publications/the-magenta-book

Hobsbawm, E. 1978 'The forward march of labour halted?,' *Marxism Today*, September. http://banmarchive.org.uk/collections/mt/pdf/78_09_hobsbawm.pdf

Hopwood, A. and Miller, P. (eds) 1994 *Accounting as Social and Institutional Practice*. Cambridge: Cambridge University Press.

International Financial Reporting Standards (IFRS) Foundation 2015 'Conceptual framework: Elements of financial statements— definitions and recognition.' August. https://www.ifrs.org/content/dam/ifrs/project/conceptual-framework/webcast-2015/cf-webcast-5-pdf.pdf

International Financial Reporting Standards (IFRS) Foundation 2018 'Conceptual framework for financial reporting.' March. https://www.ifrs.org/content/dam/ifrs/publications/pdf-standards/english/2021/issued/part-a/conceptual-framework-for-financial-reporting.pdf

Keeling, K. 2019 'Queer times, black futures,' in *Queer Times, Black Futures*. New York: New York University Press, 2019.

Keynes, J.M. 1930 *A Treatise on Money*. London: Macmillan.

Keynes, J.M. 1933 'A Monetary Theory of Production,' reprinted in D. Moggridge (ed.) *Collected Writings of John Maynard Keynes*, Vol. XIII, The General Theory and After, Part 1, ' Presentation.' London: Macmillan, 1973.

Keynes, J.M. 1936 *The General Theory of Employment, Interest and Money*. London: Macmillan.

Kockelman, P. 2006 'A semiotic ontology of the commodity,' *Journal of Linguistic Anthropology*, Vol.16, No.1.

Land, N. 2018 'Crypto-Current: Bitcoin and Philosophy.' Version 1.0, October 31. https://etscrivner.github.io/cryptocurrent/

Lazzarato, M. 2015 *Signs and Machines: Capitalism and the Production of Subjectivity*. Los Angeles: Semiotext(e).

Lee, B. 2020 'Volatility,' in Borch, C. and Wosnitzer, R. (eds) *Routledge Handbook of Critical Financial Studies*. London: Routledge.

Lee, B. and Martin, R. (eds) 2016 *Derivatives and the Wealth of Societies*. Chicago: University of Chicago Press.

Levy, J. 2014 'Accounting for profit and the history of capital,' *Critical Historical Studies*, Vol.1, No.2.

Lucarelli, S. and Gobbi, L. 2016 'Local clearing unions as stabilizers of local economic systems: a stock flow consistent perspective,' *Cambridge Journal of Economics*, Vol.40, No.5.

Mallett, J. 2020 'Scaling and consensus in monetary systems.' https://assets.pubpub.org/i0dxgael/21581338973988.pdf

Manning, E. 2021 *For a Pragmatics of the Useless*. Durham: Duke University Press.

Marazzi, C. 2011 *Capital and Affects: The Politics of the Language Economy*. Translated by Mecchia, G.. London: Semitext(e).

Martin, R. 2013a 'After economy? Social logics of the derivative,' *Social Text*, Vol.31, No.1.

Martin, R. 2013 'Dance and finance – Social kinesthetics and derivative logics,' 9 October. https://vimeo.com/95306125.

Martin, R. 2014a 'Contingent optionality. A portrait of a philosopher.' https://vimeo.com/127505126

Martin, R. 2014b 'What difference do derivatives make?,' *Culture Unbound: Journal of Current Cultural Research*, Vol.6. https://doi.org/10.3384/cu.2000.1525.146189

Martin, R. 2015 *Knowledge LTD: Towards a Social Logic of the Derivative*. Philadelphia: Temple University Press.

Marx, K. 1854 *The German Ideology*. https://www.marxists.org/archive/marx/works/download/Marx_The_German_Ideology.pdf

Marx, K. 1867 *Capital: A Critique of Political Economy*, Vol.I. https://www.marxists.org/archive/marx/works/1867-c1/

Marx, K. 1885 *Capital: A Critique of Political Economy*, Vol.II. https://www.marxists.org/archive/marx/works/1885-c2/index.htm

Marx, K. 1939 *Grundrisse*. Harmondsworth: Penguin, 1972.

Massumi, B. 2018 *99 Theses on Revaluation of Value: A Postcapitalist Manifesto*. Minnesota: University of Minnesota Press. https://uminnpressblog.com/2018/09/13/occupy-surplus-value-toward-the-revaluation-of-value/

Mayer-Schönberger, V. and Ramge, T. 2018 *Reinventing Capitalism in the Age of Big Data*. New York: Basic Books.

McLeay, M. Radia, A. and Thomas, R. (Bank of England) 2014, 'Money creation in the modern economy,' *Bank of England Quarterly Bulletin*, Q1. https://www.bankofengland.co.uk/quarterly-bulletin/2014/q1/money-creation-in-the-modern-economy

Mehrling, P. 2011a 'A Money View of the FCIC Report: Part One,' January 30. Institute for New Economic Thinking. https://www.ineteconomics.org/perspectives/blog/a-money-view-of-the-fcic-report-part-one

Mehrling, P. 2011b *The New Lombard Street: How the Fed Became the Dealer of Last Resort*. Princeton, N.J.: Princeton University Press.

Mehrling, P. n.d. 'Economics of Money and Banking,' Columbia University. https://www.coursera.org/learn/money-banking; https://en.wikipedia.org/wiki/Perry_Mehrling

Meister, R. 2021 *Justice is an Option: A Democratic Theory of Finance for the Twenty-First Century*. Chicago: University of Chicago Press.

Melamed, J. 2015 'Racial capitalism,' *Critical Ethnic Studies*, Vol.1, No.1.

Miller, M. S. 2006 *Robust Composition: Towards a Unified Approach to Access Control and Concurrency Control*. A dissertation submitted to Johns Hopkins University. https://papers.agoric.com/assets/pdf/papers/robust-composition.pdf

Miller, M. S., Van Cutsem, T. and Tulloh, B. 2013 'Distributed electronic rights in JavaScript,' in Felleisen, M. and Gardner, P. (eds.) ESOP 2013, LNCS 7792,. Springer-Verlag: Berlin Heidelberg. https://papers.agoric.com/assets/pdf/papers/distributed-electronic-rights-in-javascript.pdf

Minsky, H. 1986 *Stabilizing An Unstable Economy*. New York McGraw Hill. Reissued with commentaries. http://digamo.free.fr/minsky86.pdf

Morozov, E. 2019 'Digital socialism: The calculation debate in the age of big data,' *New Left Review*, 116/117, March. https://newleftreview.org/issues/II116/articles/evgeny-morozov-digital-socialism

Nakomoto, S. 2008 'Bitcoin: A Peer-to-Peer Electronic Cash System.' https://bitcoin.org/bitcoin.pdf

Negri, A. 1988 *Revolution Retrieved – Writings on Marx, Keynes, Capitalist Crisis and New Social Subjects*. London: Red Notes.

Orléan, A. 2014 *The Empire of Value: A New Foundation for Economics*. Translated by DeBevoise, M. Cambridge: The MIT Press.

Phillips L. and Rozworski, M. 2019 *The People's Republic of Walmart: How the World's Biggest Corporations are Laying the Foundation for Socialism*. London: Verso.

Posner, E. and Weyl, E. 2018 *Radical Markets: Uprooting Capitalism and Democracy for a Just Society*. Princeton: Princeton University Press.

Robinson, C.J. 2020 *Black Marxism*. Revised and updated third edition: *The Making of the Black Radical Tradition*. Chapel Hill: University of North Carolina Press.

Saeidinezhad, E. 2020 'Promises to pay all the way down: A primer on the money view.' https://lpeproject.org/blog/promises-all-the-way-down-a-primer-on-the-money-view.

Saros, D. 2014 *Information Technology and Socialist Construction: The End of Capital and the Transition to Socialism*. London: Routledge.

Scholes M. 1997 'Derivatives in a Dynamic Environment,' Nobel Lecture, December 9. https://www.nobelprize.org/uploads/2018/06/scholes-lecture.pdf

Sraffa, P. 1932 'Dr. Hayek on money and capital,' *The Economic Journal*, Vol.42, No.165.

Sraffa, P. 1960 *Production of Commodities By Means of Commodities: Prelude to a Critique of Economic Theory*. Cambridge: Cambridge University Press.

Stallmann, R. 1997 'The Right to Read.' *Communications of the ACM*, Vol.40, No.2. https://www.gnu.org/philosophy/right-to-read.html

Szabo, N. 1997 'The idea of smart contracts.' https://www.fon.hum.uva.nl/rob/Courses/InformationInSpeech/CDROM/Literature/LOTwinterschool2006/szabo.best.vwh.net/idea.html. Reprinted in Szabo, N. 'Essays, papers, and concise tutorials.' https://www.fon.hum.uva.nl/rob/Courses/InformationInSpeech/CDROM/Literature/LOTwinterschool2006/szabo.best.vwh.net/index.html

Tarde, G. 1902 *La Psychologie Économique*. Paris: Félix Alcan Éditeur. https://archive.org/details/sc_0000284139_00000000460844/page/n9/mode/2up

Toporowski, J. 2010 'The wisdom of property and the politics of the middle classes,' *Monthly Review*, Vol.62, No.4.

Treynor, J. 1987 'The economics of the dealer function,' *Financial Analysts Journal*, Vol.43, No.6.

Virno, P. 2003 *A Grammar of the Multitude. For an Analysis of Contemporary Forms of Life*. Translated by Bertoletti, I., Cascaito, J. and Casson, A. London: Semiotext(e).

Virno, P. 2008 *Multitude Between Innovation and Negation*. Translated by Bertoletti, I., Cascaito, J. and Casson, A. London: Semiotext(e).

Virtanen, A. 2006 'General intellect.' ECSA economic ideas. An excerpt from *Arbitrary Power. Towards a Critique of Biopolitical Economy.* Translated by Greenhill, J. Tutkijaliitto, Helsinki. https://hackmd.io/@econaut6/HkdzRAE0s

Walden, J. 2020 'The ownership economy: crypto & the next frontier of consumer software,' 14 July. https://variant.fund/articles/the-ownership-economy-crypto-and-consumer-software

Wenger, A. 2016 'Crypto tokens and the coming age of protocol innovation.' Continuations-blog, 28 July. http://continuations.com/post/148098927445/crypto-tokens-and-the-coming-age-of-protocol

Wilson, F. 2017 'Decentralized self-organizing systems.' AVC-Blog, 9 April. https://avc.com/2017/04/decentralized-self-organizing-systems

Whitehead, A. 2010 *Process and Reality.* New York: Free Press.

Zuboff, S. 2019 *The Age of Surveillance Capitalism: The Fight for a Human Future at the New Frontier of Power.* New York: Public Affair.

Ingram Content Group UK Ltd.
Milton Keynes UK
UKHW010217100523
421505UK00002B/5